step-by-step to BETTER CROCHET

a complete course of techniques with projects

Marshall Cavendish · London New York Sydney

Edited by Dorothea Hall
Art editor : Anita Ruddell

Published by Marshall Cavendish Books Limited
58 Old Compton Street
London W1V 5PA

© Marshall Cavendish Limited 1978, 1979, 1980

This material has previously appeared in the
partwork *Stitch by Stitch*.

First printing 1980

Printed in Great Britain
by Redwood Burn Limited

ISBN 0 85685 789 0

Contents

Crochet Introduction

Crochet has the great advantage of being very portable, money-saving and an immensely satisfying pastime. With a simple hook and yarn you can create fashion items for you and your family or furnishings for your home. Beginners will find these step-by-step courses clear and practical and an invaluable source of reference, while for those who are more experienced in crochet there are many fascinating new stitches and professional ideas for you to use.

Here, in twenty-nine graded courses, all the standard crochet techniques and more advanced skills are clearly explained. You are shown how to control your crochet hook and yarn, master stitches, techniques, tension, making-up and pattern adaptation, and how to apply these skills correctly and with confidence. Information is also given on making squares, circles and wheels, on working with colours in striped, chevron and checked patterns and on using unusual yarns like lurex and bouclé.

Each course is clearly illustrated with step-by-step photographs and has a special pattern for you to make as you practise the stitches and techniques. The patterns range from a simple cushion set to a beautiful rosy bed-spread, and from a child's Aran sweater to a lacy-look shawl. There is a favourite for all ages, from fashion wear to baby wear.

Step-by-step course -1

* The basis of crochet
* Making a double-crochet fabric
* Joining in a new ball of yarn
* Checking stitch tension
* Scatter cushions to make

Crochet is one of the most versatile and exciting skills to learn. If you need some inspiration, look at the samples on this page . . . just a few of the beautiful modern and traditional patterns you can create. Once you've mastered the basic stitches, it's an easy skill to develop and very quick to work.

Hooks

Crochet hooks are made in a range of sizes from a 0.60, used for fine lace crochet, to a 7.00, used in conjunction with thick yarns. The size is a metric measurement taken round the body of the shaft. All British manufacturers conform to this method of sizing, known as the International Size Range and sometimes shown as ISR in the instructions.

Yarns

Most yarns can be used for crochet, from the very fine cottons used in lace crochet to the really thick, knobbly yarns. It is best to buy all the yarn you will need for a particular design at the same time, to ensure that all the balls come from the same dye-lot; colours from different dye-lots vary considerably and this will show up badly on the finished fabric. Yarn is now sold in grammes rather than ounces, and is usually packed in 20, 25, 40, 50 or 100 gramme balls.

Alan Duns

The basis of crochet

1   To make a slip loop, first wind the yarn around your fingers like this.

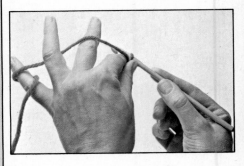

5   Wind the yarn over the left-hand fingers. This is the recommended way, but as you practise you will find your own most comfortable position.

Making a double crochet fabric

Double crochet is the smallest stitch used in crochet. It gives a firm, closely woven fabric, with a pretty, seeded appearance, which looks equally attractive worked in a fine or chunky yarn.

Before beginning to work any crochet stitches extra chain are made in order to bring the hook up to the same height as the stitch being worked and to give the fabric a straight edge. They are always counted as the first stitch of every row and are called *turning chain*.

4   Wind the yarn clockwise round the hook as before.

2

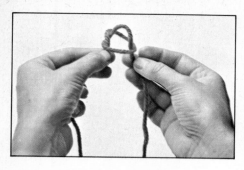

2 Slide a length of yarn through the first loop.

3 Pull through the yarn to form the slip loop. Put the loop on the crochet hook and pull it tight.

4 Hold the hook in your right hand as you would a pencil, keeping the thumb and first finger as close to the hook as possible. Rest the hook against the second finger, keeping the shank firm.

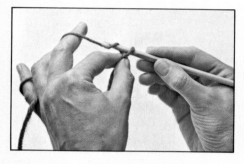

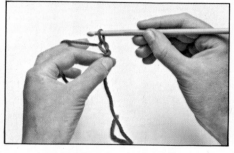

6 Hold the slip loop firmly in the left hand and wind the yarn in a clockwise direction over the shaft and round the hook.

7 Draw the yarn through the loop on the hook. This makes one chain stitch.

8 Repeat steps 6 and 7 to make as many chains as you need. Always hold the chain as close to the hook as possible with the thumb and first finger of the left hand.

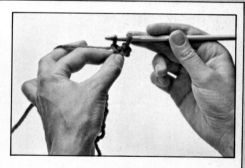

1 Make any length of chain. Insert the hook from front to back into the third chain from hook. The two missed chain are the turning chain.

2 Wind the yarn clockwise round the hook.

3 Draw the loop through the chain. There are now two loops on the hook.

5 Draw the yarn through the two loops on the hook. One double crochet made.

6 Insert the hook from front to back into the next chain.

7 Repeat steps 2 to 5 to make a double crochet.

continued

David Levin   Paul Williams

8 Continue to work one double crochet into each chain until you reach the end of the row.

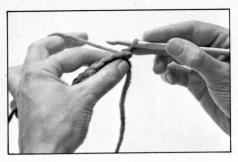

9 To turn your work keep the hook in the right hand and turn the crochet over from right to left.

10 Work one turning chain, which counts as the first stitch. Miss first stitch of previous row and work into second stitch to keep edge of work straight.

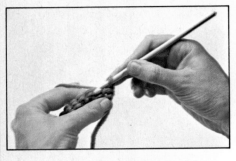

11 Insert hook from front to back into the second stitch *under* the two horizontal loops at the top.

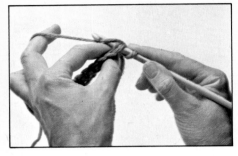

12 Wind the yarn round the hook as in step 2.

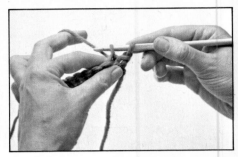

13 Draw through the loop as in step 3.

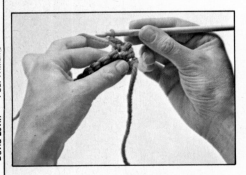

14 Wind yarn over hook again and pull through to complete the first double crochet of the new row. Repeat to end.

15 Work the last double crochet into the turning chain of the previous row. Do this on every row to keep the edge straight.

16 After working required rows, fasten off by drawing yarn through last loop at end of row. Pull tight, break off yarn, darn in loose end with wool needle.

Keeping the edge straight

When you begin working a crochet fabric you may find it difficult to keep the edges straight. Don't worry – this is a common mistake. It happens because you are not working into the correct stitches at each end of the row. Remember to make a turning chain at the beginning of the row, work into the second stitch, missing the first stitch as in step 11. Work the last stitch into the turning chain at the end of the row as in step 15.

1 The fabric will slant inwards if you do not work into the turning chain at the end of the row.

2 The fabric will get wider if you do not miss the first stitch and work into the second stitch.

Joining in a new ball of yarn

A new ball of yarn should always be joined into the fabric at the side of the work, and never in the middle of a row. If you reach the middle of the row and have insufficient yarn to complete it, take the hook out of the working loop and unravel the yarn back to the side edge. Pick up the working loop to join in the new yarn. Remedy mistakes by unravelling the yarn in the same way.

1 Work to the end of the row in the usual way until the two loops of the last stitch are on the hook.

2 Hold the fabric and yarn in left hand and loop the new yarn round the hook.

3 Draw new yarn through the two loops on hook. This completes the stitch and introduces the new yarn.

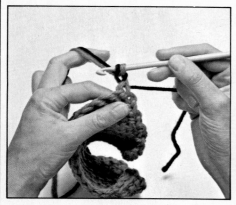

4 Turn work. Hold the old and new yarn together and work the turning chain with both yarns together to hold the new yarn in place. Pull the loose ends to tighten the stitch.

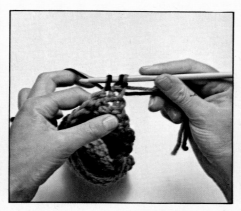

5 Work the next stitch using the new yarn alone.

6 Continue working with new yarn. When you have finished the piece come back to the two loose ends and darn in, using a blunt-ended wool needle.

Stitch tension

To make sure that your crochet is the correct measurement when completed, it is advisable to work a tension square in the hook and yarn stated to check your tension. If necessary you can alter the number of stitches by changing the hook size. Keep changing the hook size until your tension is correct.

Example: Your instructions quote 12 stitches to 10cm on a No. 5.50 hook using a chunky yarn. Make a piece with at least 24 stitches, not less than 10cm deep. Count up 12 stitches and mark with pins. Pin the piece flat and measure your 12 stitches.

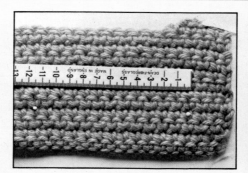

If the 12 stitches measure more than 10cm your tension is too loose and you must change to a smaller hook.

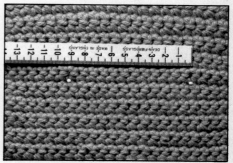

If the 12 stitches measure less than 10cm your tension is too tight and you must change to a larger hook.

Scatter cushions

Practice your stitches on one of these simple cushions or, maybe two or three . . . a colourful collection for your house or garden.

Size :
We give specific instructions to fit a cushion pad 41cm [16in] square (available from most needlecraft departments).

Materials
For 1 cover in double knitting yarn
  approx 180g
4.00mm crochet hook
For 1 cover in chunky knitting yarn
  approx 300g
5.50mm crochet hook
1 cushion pad 41cm square for each
  cushion
1   Make 69 chain for double knitting yarn or 55 chain for chunky knitting yarn.
2   Continue working in rows of double crochet, with 68 double crochet in each row for double knitting, or 54 in each row for chunky knitting yarn.
3   Work until fabric measures 38cm from beginning. Fasten off.
4   Darn in all loose ends of yarn using a blunt-ended wool needle. Make another piece in the same way.
5   Using either the same double knitting yarn, or a thinner yarn in a matching colour for chunky knitting yarn, oversew round three sides of cushion.
6   Insert cushion pad into cover. Oversew remaining seam.

☐ To calculate the size of cover for an existing cushion, measure the width and depth of your cushion and make the cover 2.5cm *less* all round. **Example** : for a cushion measuring 35.5cm square you will need a 33cm-square cover.

☐ To work out the number of stitches for any size cover : make a sample piece measuring approximately 10cm square, in the stitch and yarn you are using. Measure 5cm with a ruler and count the number of stitches. **Example** : if you have 10 stitches to 5cm (i.e. 2 stitches to 1cm) you will need to make 66 chain plus two extra for the turning chain, for a 33cm cover.

Step-by-step course – 2

Making a half treble fabric

1 Make any length of chain. Wind yarn clockwise round the hook.

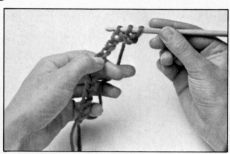

2 Insert the hook from front to back into the third chain from the hook. First two are turning chain.

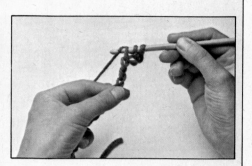

3 Wind the yarn round the hook.

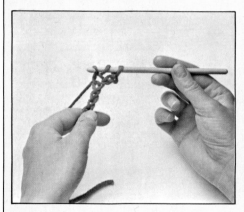

4 Draw the yarn through the chain. There are now three loops on the hook.

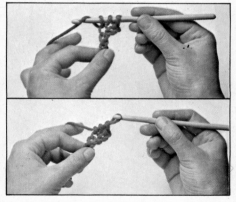

5 Wind the yarn round the hook and draw it through all three loops on the hook. One half treble has been made.

6 Repeat these actions into each chain to the end.

7 Turn work. Make **two** turning chain.

8 Miss the first stitch. Work the first half-treble as before into the second stitch. Work one half-treble into each stitch to the end of the row.

9 Work the last half-treble into the turning chain of the previous row. Repeat these last three steps for the number of rows you require.

David Levin   Paul Williams

7

The cosy baby bag

Warm as toast for chilly days – a snug sleeping bag worked in half trebles.

John Hawkins/Baby Carrier—Harrods

of row. Work last half-treble into turning chain of previous row. Turn.

Continue working in rows of half-treble in this way until back measures 56cm. Draw yarn through and fasten off.

Left front
Using No. 5.50mm hook make 18 chain. Work 1 half-treble into 3rd chain from hook, 1 half-treble into each chain to end. Turn. 17 half-treble.

Continue working in rows of half-treble as given for back.

Work until left front measures same as back. Draw yarn through and fasten off.

Right front
Using No. 5.50mm hook make 24 chain. Work 1 half-treble into 3rd chain from hook, 1 half-treble into each chain to end. Turn. 23 half-treble.

Continue working in rows of half-treble until right front measures same as back. Draw yarn through and fasten off.

Sleeves
Using No. 5.50mm hook make 24 chain. Work 1 half-treble into each chain to end of row. 23 half-treble.

Continue working in half-treble until sleeve measures 13.5cm. Draw yarn through and fasten off.

Base
Using No. 5.50mm hook make 9 chain. Work 1 half-treble into 3rd chain from hook, 1 half-treble into each chain to end. Turn. 8 half-trebles.

Continue working in rows of half-treble until piece measures 34cm. Draw yarn through and fasten off.

To make up
☐ With right sides of work facing, pin back and front pieces together with right front overlapping left front by approximately 5cm.

☐ Using a flat seam throughout join right and left shoulder seams for 9cm at each side. Mark a point 9cm from shoulder on side seams for armholes. With right sides facing sew sleeve tops in position along armhole opening.

☐ Join side and sleeve seams.

☐ Join right front to left front on the right side, for 9cm from bottom edge where they overlap. Sew the left front to the right front on the wrong side in the same way.

☐ Pin the base to the bottom of the bag matching side seams to centre of base ends.

☐ Sew in place using a flat seam.

☐ Sew two poppers at the inner and outer edge of the left front at the neck edge to hold in place. Repeat 3 more times at even intervals down the front opening.

☐ Thread ribbon through the last row of half trebles on the sleeves and draw up. Tie a bow at neck edge on right front at same place as poppers if required.

Diagram measurements:

- sleeve
- back — 56cm × 34cm
- 21.5 cm × 13.5 cm
- right front — 56cm × 21.5 cm
- left front — 56cm × 15 cm
- base — 34 cm × 7.5 cm

Size:
To fit a baby up to 6 months. Length to shoulder, 56cm. Sleeve seam, 13.5cm.

Tension
11 stitches and 9 rows to 10cm over half-treble worked on a No. 5.50mm hook.

Materials
300g Peter Pan Darling Chunky
1 No. 5.50mm crochet hook
8 poppers (press studs)
Ribbon for trimming

Back
Using No. 5.50mm hook make 38 chain. Work 1 half-treble into 3rd chain from hook, then 1 half-treble into each chain to end. Turn, 37 half-treble worked.
Next row work 2 chain to count as 1st half-treble, miss 1st stitch, work a half-treble into next and every stitch to end

Step-by-step course - 3

*Understanding correct tension
*How to check tension
*Using a substitute yarn

Understanding correct tension

Now that you have mastered the basic stitches in crochet it is vital to understand the importance of obtaining the 'correct tension' when working a pattern, as this can mean the difference between success and failure.

Most people think that tension refers to the ability to be able to make a smooth, even fabric, but this is not so. By 'correct tension' we mean working the same number of stitches and rows to a given measurement as the pattern designer

used. This is usually worked out over 10cm. Remember that although you may not get the same number of stitches to begin with, this does not mean that your tension is 'wrong', but simply that you work either slightly more loosely or tightly than the designer. This difference can easily be remedied by changing to a different size hook.

Before beginning to work on a pattern the designer will crochet a square using the hook, yarn and stitch intended for the garment. The number of stitches in this square will determine the size and shape of the finished garment as all the measure-

ments for it will be calculated from this figure. So, unless your tension is the same as in the instructions the garment will not turn out the same size as the original. Remember that a difference of even half a stitch over 10cm can alter the size of the finished fabric.

It is sometimes difficult to achieve the correct tension in both the stitches and rows, but it is more important to get the number of stitches right, since this determines the garment width. It is much easier to control the length of the garment, simply by working more or fewer rows, as necessary.

Checking your tension

The tension quoted for this sample is 15 stitches and 13 rows over half treble worked in double knitting yarn using a 4.00mm hook.

1 Make a tension square using a hook, yarn and stitch given in the tension, but work a few extra stitches.

2 The tension is gauged over 10cm, so make a square at least 10cm square to be able to check it correctly.

3 Pin the piece out on to a flat surface without stretching the stitches.

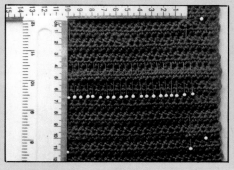

4 This sample has only 13 stitches to 10cm instead of the 15 quoted, so change to a smaller hook.

5 This sample has 19 stitches to 10cm, which is too many, so change to a larger hook.

6 Keep on changing to a smaller or larger hook until you achieve the correct tension as in this sample.

Paul Williams

Using a substitute yarn

If you are unable to buy the particular yarn quoted in your instructions it is sometimes possible to use a substitute,

but it must be as near a match as possible.

To check your tension, work a 10cm square using the stitch and hook suggested, and measure to see if you need a larger or smaller hook size. If, by chang-

ing the hook size, you are able to obtain exactly the same tension as quoted it is all right to go ahead with the substitute yarn, although the garment will, of course, look and feel different from the original.

Step-by-step course – 4

* Making a treble fabric
* Joining with double crochet
* Scarf patterns

Making a treble fabric

A treble is the first of the long stitches used so frequently in crochet. It makes a more open fabric than double crochet and when used with fine yarns can produce a lattice effect. In filet crochet, for example, blocks of trebles are worked to form different motifs over an open lattice background. They can also be used in conjunction with double crochet and half-trebles to make shaped motifs such as shells.

Since the treble is a much longer stitch than a double crochet it is necessary to work three turning chain at the beginning of every row. Work the last stitch of every row into the top of the three turning chain of the previous row to keep the edge straight, and to prevent the yarn from pulling the work out of shape at the side edge.

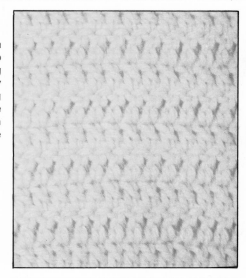

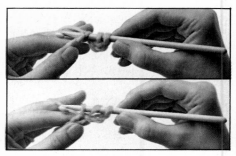

1 Make any number of chain, making two more chain than the number of stitches you will need, i.e. for 30 stitches make 32 chain. Wind the yarn round the hook. Insert the hook from front to back into fourth chain from hook.
2 Wind the yarn round the hook and draw through a loop. Three loops on hook.

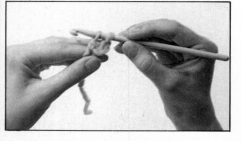

3 Wind the yarn round the hook and draw it through the first two loops on the hook. Two loops remain on hook.

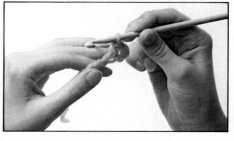

4 Wind the yarn round the hook and draw it through the last two loops on the hook. One treble made.

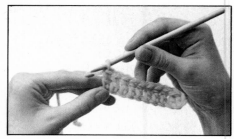

5 Work one treble in the same way into each chain to the end of the row.

6 Turn work. Work three turning chain. Miss the first stitch. Work the first treble into the second stitch.

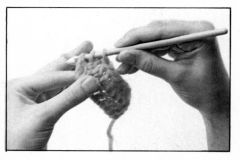

7 Work into each treble to end, work the last treble into the top of the turning chain of the previous row.

8 Continue to work in this way for the number of rows you need. Fasten off.

Paul Williams

Joining with double crochet

A decorative seam can be made by joining two pieces of fabric with double crochet. Make a feature of the seam by using a contrast-colour yarn. When worked on the wrong side of the fabric the seam gives a laced appearance on the right side.

1 Pin together two pieces of fabric to be joined just below the edge of the seam.

2 Insert hook through both thicknesses of fabric.

3 Loop the yarn round the hook and draw it through.

4 Work one chain with both ends of yarn and pull firmly to hold it in place.

5 Work one chain, one double crochet into next row end just below the edge.

6 Continue to work one double crochet into each row end to the end of the seam. Draw yarn through and fasten off.

7 When working with a treble fabric, work three stitches into every two row ends.

8 One chain can be worked between each stitch to spread the stitches along the seam.

Paul Williams

Scarves for all the family

Scarves that look good on all ages, worked in double knitting wool, using the stitches you have learnt so far. Turn back the bottom to make pockets joined with a decorative double crochet seam, or fold the scarf in half and join the two edges at the centre to make a cosy hood.

Scarf with pockets

Adult's scarf measures 20cm wide x 170cm long with pockets turned back.
Child's scarf measures 17cm wide x 122cm long with pockets turned back.

Tension
17sts and 10 rows to 10cm over treble worked on a 4.00mm hook.

Note follow the figures in brackets [] for the adult's scarf.

George Wright/accessories Fenwicks

Materials
*8[10] 25g balls of double knitting
yarn such as Sirdar Superwash Double
Knitting.
4.00mm hook.
Small quantity of contrast colour
yarn (optional).*

To make scarf
Using a 4.00mm hook make 30 [36]
chain.
☐ Work 1 treble into 4th chain from hook,
1 tr into each chain to end of row. 28 [34]
treble.
☐ Continue working in rows of treble
working 3 turning chain at the beginning
of every row until work measures
154.5 [219]cm or the length you require.
Fasten off. Darn in all ends.

To make pockets
Turn 14.5 [23]cm up at each end to form
pockets and pin into place.
Join the pockets with double crochet.
☐ Work from right to left with the pocket
facing you and folded edge to the right.
Using a 4.00mm hook and contrast-
colour yarn, insert hook from front to
back through both thicknesses of scarf.
Loop the yarn over the hook and draw
a loop through. Work 1 chain using both
ends of yarn to hold the stitch in place.
Now work with 1 end of yarn only,
work *1 chain, 1 double crochet into
the next row end. Repeat from * to the end
of the pocket, working the last double
crochet into the corner of the pocket.
☐ Work the other side of the pocket in the
same way, but beginning from the top
edge of the pocket so that the front of the
double crochet shows on the same side of
the pocket.
☐ Work the other pocket in the same way.
Darn in all ends.
☐ Press the scarf according to the
instructions on the ball band.

Scarf with hood

Size
Adult's scarf measures 23cm wide x
162cm long.
Child's scarf measures 17cm wide x
142.5cm long.

Tension
17sts and 12½ rows to 10cm over double
crochet worked on a 4.00mm hook.

Materials
*7[11]x25g balls of double knitting yarn
4mm crochet hook*
Note follow the figures in brackets []
for the adult's scarf.

To make scarf
Using a 4.00mm hook make 30 [41]
chain.
☐ Work 1 double crochet into 3rd chain
from hook, 1 double crochet into each
chain to end. 29 [40] double crochet.
☐ *Work in rows of 3cm double
crochet, 5cm half-treble, 7cm treble,
5cm half-treble. Repeat from * until work
measures 142.5 [162]cm or length you
require, ending with 3cm double crochet.
Fasten off. Darn in all ends.
☐ Fold the scarf in half and pin seam
together at centre for 18 [22]cm to form
hood.

To join with double crochet
☐ Insert the hook from front to back at
centre fold through both thicknesses of
the scarf just below the edge of the seam.
Loop the yarn over the hook and draw
the yarn through. Wind 2 thicknesses
of yarn round hook and draw through
the loop to hold the yarn in place.
Continue working through both
thicknesses working 2 double crochet
into each row end, for 18 [22]cm.
Draw yarn through and fasten off.
Darn in all ends.
☐ Press the scarf according to the
instructions on the ball band.

George Wright/accessories Fenwicks

Step-by-step course – 5

Double and triple trebles, sometimes known as long trebles, are two of the longest of the crochet stitches and are made by winding the yarn two or three times round the hook before beginning to work the stitch.

When worked in a thick yarn they produce an open, chunky fabric that is very quick to make. They are more frequently used in fine lace crochet with other stitches to form either an openwork fabric or an interesting pattern.

It is important to remember that the turning chain must be lengthened to bring the hook up to the height of the stitch being worked; four chain are worked for a double treble and five for a triple treble. The chain counts as the first stitch.

Making a double treble fabric

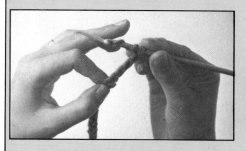

1 Make any length of chain, making three more chain than the number of stitches you require, e.g. for ten stitches make 13 chain. Wind the yarn clockwise twice round the hook.

2 Insert the hook from front to back in to the fifth chain from the hook.

3 Wind the yarn clockwise round the hook.

4 Draw a loop through. There are now four loops on the hook.

5 Wind the yarn clockwise round the hook and draw it through the first two loops on the hook. Three loops left on the hook.

6 Wind the yarn clockwise round the hook and draw through the next two loops on the hook. Two loops left on hook.

7 Wind the yarn clockwise round the hook and draw it through the last two loops on the hook. One double treble has been made.

8 Work one double treble in the same way into each chain to end. Turn.

9 Make four turning chain.

Paul Williams

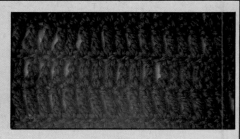

10 Miss the first stitch. Work one double treble into the second stitch, working under the two horizontal loops in the normal way.

11 Work one double treble into each stitch to the end of the row. Work the last double treble into the top of the turning chain of the previous row.

12 Repeat the last three steps for as many rows as you require. Draw the yarn through the loop and fasten off.

Making a triple treble fabric

1 Make any length of chain, making four more chain than the number of stitches you require, e.g. for 12 stitches make 16 chain. Wind yarn clockwise three times round the hook.

2 Insert the hook from front to back into the sixth chain from the hook. Wind yarn round the hook and draw through a loop. Five loops on the hook.

3 Wind yarn round the hook and draw through first two loops. Four loops on the hook.

4 Repeat step 3 twice more. Two loops left on the hook.

5 Wind yarn round the hook and draw through last two loops on the hook. One triple treble made.

6 Work one triple treble in same way into each chain to end. Turn. Work five turning chain.

7 Miss the first stitch. Work one triple treble into second stitch, working under two horizontal loops in the normal way.

8 Work one triple treble into each stitch to end. Work last triple treble into the top of the turning chain of the previous row.

9 Repeat the last three steps for the number of rows required. Draw yarn through and fasten off.

Fisherman's smock

Get out and about in this simply styled cotton fisherman's smock. With draw-string waist and side-opening pocket it is made in double treble stitch – the sleeves and yoke are worked straight across from cuff to cuff.

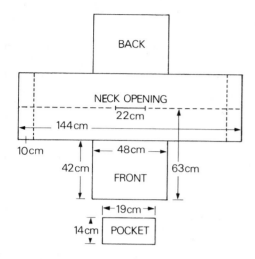

Size
To fit 87/92cm bust.
Length to shoulder, 63cm.
Sleeve seam, 48cm.
To make the top bigger add approximately 3 stitches for every extra 2cm to be added.

Tension
13 sts and 5½ rows to 10cm worked over double trebles on a 4.00mm hook.

Materials
650g of 3 Suisses Alezan Cotton
4.00 mm crochet hook

Back
Using 4.00mm hook make 65 chain.
Work 1 double treble into 5th chain from hook, then 1 double treble into each chain to end. Turn. 62 double trebles.
☐ Continue to work in rows of double treble with 4 turning chain at beginning of every row until piece measures 42cm from beginning.
☐ Draw yarn through and fasten off.

Front
Work in same way as for back.

Sleeves and yoke (worked in one piece)
Begin at cuff, work first sleeve, yoke, then second sleeve and end at cuff.
☐ Using 4.00mm hook make 62 chain. Work first row as given for back. back until piece measures 61cm, ending
☐ Work in rows of double treble as for back until sleeve measures 61cm, ending at right-hand edge of right side of work. This will be the lower edge of front yoke.

Shape neck
Work in double treble on first 29 stitches only for front neck, leaving remaining 29 stitches unworked. Continue for 22cm, ending at neck edge. Fasten off. Return to the last complete row worked.
☐ Rejoin yarn to remaining stitches at neck edge and work back yoke on these stitches, working the same number of rows as for front, ending at the *side edge*. Turn.
☐ Work across 29 stitches of back yoke, then across the 29 stitches of front yoke. 58 sts.
☐ Complete the yoke and sleeve on these stitches.
☐ Continue for a further 61cm. Draw yarn through and fasten off.

To make pocket
Using 4.00mm hook make 19 chain.
☐ Work 1 half treble into 3rd chain from hook, 1 half treble into each chain to end. Turn. 18 half trebles.
☐ Work 19cm on these stitches. Draw yarn through and fasten off.

To make up
Darn in all loose ends of yarn on wrong side of work.
☐ Mark a point with coloured thread on both sleeves at front and back, 48cm from edge of cuff.
☐ Using the markers as a guide, pin the front to front yoke and the back to back yoke and sew in place using a flat seam.
☐ Join side and sleeve seams using a back stitch seam, reversing the seam for 10cm at each cuff.
☐ Work a row of double crochet all round pocket, neck edge, cuffs and welt.
☐ Sew on pocket to front at top and bottom so that openings are at the side. Turn back cuffs to right side.

To make the cord
Make a chain 117cm long.
☐ Insert hook into 2nd chain from hook and draw yarn through both loops to make 1 slip stitch. Work 1 slip stitch into each chain to end.
☐ Fasten off and darn in loose ends. Thread cord through double treble at welt and draw up.

Country-life tabard

Using double treble stitches, make this tweedy-look tabard for out-of-doors days in country or town. Made out of two simple rectangles, the shoulders are joined with fine double crochet and the sides are laced with crochet chain.

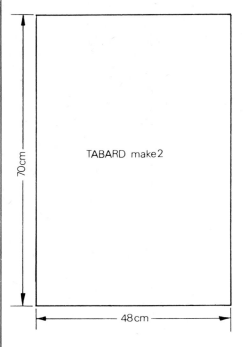

TABARD make 2

70cm

48cm

Size
The instructions given here are for a medium size, 87/92cm bust.
Length to shoulder, 70cm.
To make the tabard bigger work approximately 1 stitch more for every centimetre you wish to add.

Tension
9 stitches and 3½ rows to 10cm over double treble on a 5.50mm hook.

Materials
750g of chunky knitting yarn such as Hayfield Saxon
Small quantity of double knitting wool in a contrast colour
5.50mm hook
4.00mm hook

Front and back sections
Using chunky yarn and 5.50mm hook make 47 chain for back. Work 1 double treble into 5th chain from hook, 1 double treble into each chain to end.
☐ Continue to work in rows of double treble making 4 turning chain at the beginning of every row, until the piece measures 70cm from the beginning, measured with work flat.
Draw yarn through and fasten off.

☐ Work the front in the same way.
☐ Darn in all the loose ends on the wrong side of the work.

To work the edging
Join the chunky yarn to the right side of one piece at the shoulder edge. Work 1 chain, then 1 double crochet and 1 chain down the side edge, working into the double treble at the end of each row.
☐ Work down other side edge in the same way. Finish other piece to match.

Joining shoulders with crochet braid
By working a few rows of double crochet in a fine yarn you can obtain a braid effect on the edge of a chunky fabric and it is possible to join two pieces together by working through both the edge stitches of one piece and the braid stitches at the same time, to make a contrasting seam.
☐ With the right side of the front facing join double knitting yarn to left shoulder edge. Using 4.00mm hook make 1 chain, then work 1 double crochet and 1 chain along the shoulder edge for 13.5cm.

George Wright

Lacing of tabard in another colourway.

☐ Turn and work 1 double crochet into each double crochet and chain to the end. Work 1 more row of double crochet in to these stitches.
☐ With the right side of the back facing match the shoulder edges of front and back. Insert hook through back and through first stitch of the edging just worked. Draw the yarn through and work a double crochet in the normal way through both thicknesses.
☐ Continue working in double crochet in this way to join the shoulder together, working into the corresponding stitches of back and front. When you have reached the shoulder edge, draw yarn through and fasten off.
☐ Work the other shoulder in the same way, starting from the neck edge.
☐ Darn in all the loose ends on the wrong side of the work using a wool needle.

Joining the sides with lacing
Mark a point 26cm from shoulder edge at either side for armholes.
☐ Using double knitting yarn and 4.00mm hook make 180 chain. Draw yarn through and fasten off. Make another chain in the same way. Lace the chain through the side seams to join them for 24cm.

Optional belt
If you wish to make a belt make a chain in the chunky yarn about 170cm long and work one row of double crochet then fasten off. Make another narrow belt in the double knitting yarn making a strip by working 4 double crochet for the same length. Fasten off.
Twist them together to make the belt.

Step-by-step course – 6

*Shaping with double crochet and half trebles
*Working a slip stitch
*Baby smock patterns

Shaping with double crochet and half trebles

Because of the height of most crochet stitches, it is important to take care when increasing or decreasing a stitch at the fabric edge, otherwise the edge may not be straight and smooth. You only have to miss one stitch at the beginning or end of a row when you are decreasing a stitch to get an edge that is uneven and stepped. This is not only unattractive, but also difficult to seam and happens particularly when working with half trebles. To avoid this a single stitch is usually decreased by working two stitches together, one stitch in from the edge. It is also better to increase one stitch on the second and second to last stitch in a row, to get a really smooth edge.

To decrease one double crochet at each end of a row

1 Work 1 turning chain at the beginning of the row and miss the 1st stitch in the usual way.

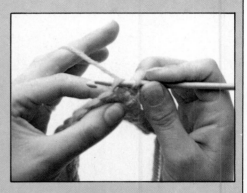

2 Insert hook from front to back into next stitch.

3 Wind yarn clockwise round hook and draw through a loop. 2 loops on hook.

4 Insert hook into next stitch. Wind yarn clockwise round hook and draw through a loop. 3 loops on hook.

5 Wind yarn round hook and draw through all 3 loops on hook. 1 stitch decreased.

6 Work in double crochet to last 3 stitches.

7 Work the next 2 stitches together by repeating steps 2 to 5.

8 Work the last stitch into the turning chain of the previous row.

To decrease one half treble at each end of a row

1 Work 2 turning chain at the beginning of the row and miss the 1st stitch in the usual way.

2 Wind yarn round hook and insert hook into next stitch.

3 Wind yarn round hook and draw through a loop. 3 loops on hook.

4 Wind yarn round hook. Insert hook into next stitch.

5 Wind yarn round hook and draw through a loop. 5 loops on hook.

6 Wind yarn round hook and draw through all 5 loops on hook. 1 stitch decreased.

7 Work 1 half treble into each stitch to last 3 stitches.

8 Work next 2 stitches together by repeating steps 2 to 6.

9 Work the last half treble into the turning chain of the previous row. 1 stitch has been decreased at each end of row.

Paul Williams

To increase one double crochet at each end of a row

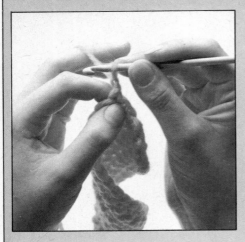

1 Work the turning chain at the beginning of the row in the usual way.

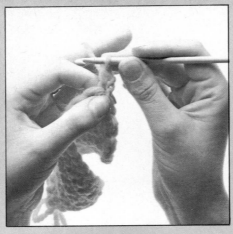

2 Miss first double crochet, work 2 double crochet into the 2nd stitch of the previous row.

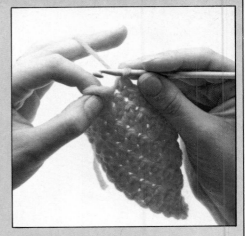

3 Continue to work into each stitch to the last 2 double crochet.

4 Work 2 double crochet into the next stitch.

5 Work the last double crochet into the turning chain of the previous row. 1 stitch has been increased at each end.

6 Work in exactly the same way for half trebles.

Working a slip stitch

It is possible to use crochet slip stitch in various ways, but however it is used the working method is always the same. Use it as a means of shaping: either by working over several stitches at the beginning of a row to decrease them, or as a means of getting from one point to another in a row (when making button-holes or shaping a neck).

Alternatively, slip stitch can be used for joining the two ends of a round when working circular motifs.

Slip stitch is seldom used on its own in a pattern, except for making a crochet cord. The shallowness of the stitch produces a firm cord, which is often used for fastening baby clothes.

To make a crochet cord

1 Make the length of chain you require. Insert the hook from front to back into the 2nd chain from hook.

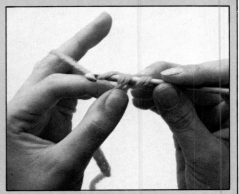

2 Wind the yarn clockwise round the hook.

continued

continued : to make a crochet cord

3 Draw a loop through both loops on the hook. 1 slip stitch made.

4 Work 1 slip stitch into each chain to the end to make the cord.

5 To make a firmer cord with a plaited appearance work 1 slip stitch into each chain along the other side.

Paul Williams

Three baby smocks

Three pretty variations on the smock theme; one with sleeves, two without, worked in double crochet and trebles. Made in a fine, soft yarn, they are either plain or striped, with easy shaping on the skirt.

Baby's smock with sleeves

Size
To fit a baby up to 6 months old.
Length from shoulder, 28.5cm, excluding contrast edging.
Sleeve seam, 15cm.

Materials
100g of Pingouin Mademoiselle 4 ply
Small quantity of contrast colour for
edging and back ties
1.75mm crochet hook
2.00mm crochet hook
Note you could make the smock striped by working every two rows in a contrasting colour.

Tension
24 stitches and 12 rows to 10cm over treble worked on a 1.75mm hook.

To make smock front
Using 1.75mm hook make 58 chain.
Work 1 treble into 4th chain from hook, 1 treble into each chain to end. 56 stitches.
□ Work 20 rows in treble crochet, increasing one stitch at each end of every row by working 1 stitch into the first stitch after the turning chain instead of missing it at the beginning of the row and 2 stitches into the 2nd to last stitch at the

Kim Sayer/Dress – Harrods

end of the row. The skirt will measure approximately 17.5cm and there will be a total of 96 stitches in all.
Draw yarn through last loop and fasten off.

To make bodice
Return to chain at beginning of skirt.
Miss first 7 chain for armhole. With right side facing, using 2.00mm hook, rejoin yarn to the 8th chain and work a row of

double crochet across the chain, working the last double crochet into the 8th chain from the end, leaving the last 7 chain for the second armhole.
□ Continue working in double crochet on these 44 stitches for 6cm.

To shape neck
Work across first 16 double crochet on next row, then turn and work on these stitches only for one side of neck.

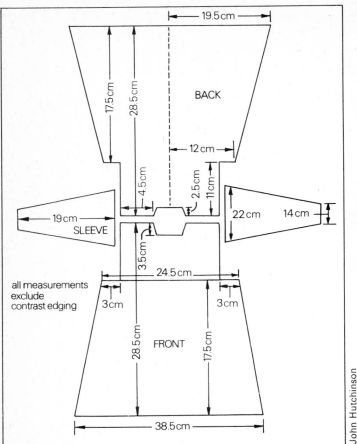

all measurements exclude contrast edging

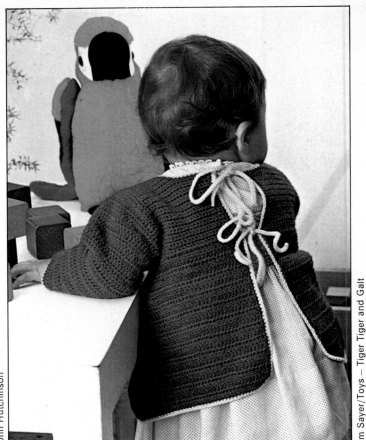

John Hutchinson

Kim Sayer/Toys – Tiger Tiger and Galt

☐ Decrease 1 stitch at the beginning of the next row for the neck edge, then continue in double crochet to the end of the row. Turn.

☐ Continue to decrease 1 stitch at the *beginning* of every alternate row in the same way until 11 stitches remain. You will be decreasing 1 stitch at the neck edge. Draw yarn through the last loop and fasten off. Return to the stitches at the centre of the bodice.

☐ With the right side of the front facing, miss the first 12 stitches for the centre neck and rejoin the yarn to the next double crochet.

☐ Complete other side of neck to match the first, decreasing 1 stitch at neck edge on every alternate row, until 11 stitches remain.

☐ Draw yarn through last loop and fasten off.

To make right back
Using 1.75mm hook make 29 chain. Work the 1st row as given for front. 27 stitches.

☐ Increase 1 stitch at the beginning of the next row as given for front. Increase 1 stitch in the same way at the same edge on every row, keeping the other edge straight for centre back opening, until skirt measures the same as the back skirt. There should be 47 stitches. Draw yarn through last loop and fasten off.

To make bodice
Return to chain at beginning of skirt.

☐ With right side of work facing and using a 2.00mm hook, rejoin yarn to 8th chain from shaped side edge, leaving the first 7 chain for armhole. Work in double crochet to end of row. 22 stitches.

☐ Continue without shaping until bodice measures 8cm from beginning, ending at armhole edge.

To shape neck
Work across first 13 double crochet on next row, turn and leave remaining stitches for back neck.

☐ Decrease 1 stitch at beginning of next and every following alternate row in the same way as for the front until 11 stitches remain and work measures the same as the front to shoulder. Draw yarn through and fasten off.

To make the left back
Work in the same way as the right back, but work increases at the end of the row instead of at the beginning, on the skirt. Miss 7 chain at the end of the row for the armhole, instead of at the beginning, to reverse the shaping. Work the neck shaping in reverse in exactly the same way.

To make the sleeves
Join shoulder seams using a back stitch seam.

☐ Using a 1.75mm hook and with right side of the front facing, rejoin yarn to inside armhole at shaped side edge. Work 1 row of double crochet up one side of yoke, to shoulder then down other side of yoke to inside edge of armhole. 58 sts. Turn. Work 2 rows in treble on these stitches.

☐ Continue working in treble, decreasing 1 stitch at beginning of every row until sleeve measures 19cm from beginning. Draw yarn through last loop and fasten off. Work 2nd sleeve in same way on other side of yoke.

To make up
Darn in all loose ends of yarn on wrong side of smock. Press lightly according to instructions on the ball band. With wrong side of work facing join top edges of sleeves to armholes at top of skirt, using a flat seam.

☐ Join side and sleeve seams using a back stitch seam.

To work edging
Using main colour and 1.75mm hook and with right side of left back facing, join yarn to corner and work a row of double crochet all round, up right back, round neck and down left back to corner, working 3 double crochet into each corner stitch and missing 1 stitch at each corner of inside neck. Draw yarn through last loop and fasten off.

To make contrast edging and ties

With right side of work facing join contrast colour yarn to same corner as before.

☐ Work 1 double crochet all round hem and up back edge to point where skirt is joined to bodice, work 65 chain, then work 1 slip stitch into each chain just worked, back to edge again. This forms first tie.

☐ Continue to work in double crochet to first neck edge corner, then work another tie in the same way.

☐ Continue to work in double crochet round neck without missing 1 stitch at inside neck edges to next back edge corner. Work another tie in the same way at this corner. Complete the edging working another tie in the same way where yoke joins skirt. Draw yarn through last loop and fasten off. Darn in all ends on wrong side of work.

Baby's sleeveless smock

Size

To fit a baby up to 6 months old.

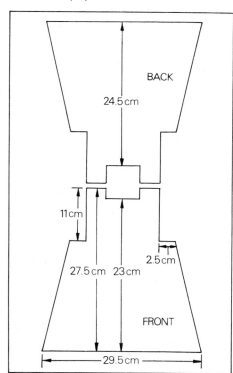

John Hutchinson

Tension

24 stitches and 12 rows to 10cm worked over treble on a 1.75mm hook.

Materials

50g of Pingouin Mademoiselle 4 ply in one colour for skirt, called A
50g of the same yarn in a contrast colour for the bodice, called B
The striped version also takes 50g of A and 50g of B
1.75mm crochet hook
2.00mm crochet hook

Steve Bicknell

Note to make the striped version work two rows in each colour down skirt, ending by working one row in the first colour used. Work the yoke all in one colour.

To make the front skirt

Using 1.75mm hook and A, make 58 chain.

☐ Work 1 treble into 4th chain from hook, 1 treble into each chain to end. Turn. 56 trebles. Continue to work in trebles, increasing 1 stitch at the beginning of every row by working 1 stitch into the first stitch after the turning chain, until the skirt measures 12.5cm from the beginning. You should have worked approximately 21 rows and have 76 stitches in all. Draw yarn through last loop and fasten off.

To make the front yoke

Return to the chain at the beginning of the skirt.

☐ With the right side of the skirt facing, using B and 2.00mm hook, rejoin yarn to the 8th chain from the side edge, leaving the first 7 chain for the armhole. Work 1 turning chain, then 1 double crochet into each chain, working the last double crochet into the 8th chain from the end, leaving the last 7 chain for the second armhole.

☐ Continue working in rows of double crochet on these stitches for 6cm. Work across first 13 double crochet, turn and work on these stitches only for 3cm.

To shape neck

Fasten off. Return to stitches at neck edge. Miss first 18 stitches for centre neck. Rejoin yarn to next stitch and complete to

match first side. Draw yarn through and fasten off.

To make the back skirt

Work exactly as given for front skirt.

To make the back yoke

Work exactly as given for front, but work for 7.5cm before shaping the neck and work for 1.5cm only for neck so that the yoke is the same depth as front yoke.

To make up

Darn all loose ends in to wrong side of work. Press pieces lightly, following instructions on the ball band. Join side seams using a flat seam.

To work edging and shoulder ties

Using 1.75mm hook, B and with right side of front facing, join yarn to underarm at side seam. Work a row of double crochet round armhole to shoulder.

☐ Work 65 chain at corner of shoulder, turn and slip stitch into each chain just worked, back to shoulder to make the first tie. Work in double crochet to next corner and work another tie in same way. Continue to work round neck in double crochet, missing 1 stitch at inside neck corners, then work across shoulders, and make a tie at each of the corners as before.

☐ Work down the armhole and round back in the same way, making 1 tie at each corner on shoulders as before. Join the last double crochet to the first double crochet worked with a slip stitch. Draw yarn through and fasten off. Darn in any loose ends on the wrong side of the work using a blunt-ended wool needle.

Step-by-step course –7

*How to shape a treble or double treble fabric
*How to increase and decrease several stitches at each end of a row
*Pattern for an evening sweater

How to shape a treble or double treble fabric

Because of the depth of both the treble and double treble stitches it is important to take care when working your shaping, in order to achieve a neat, firm edge to your fabric.

Unless a pattern specifically states the method to be used, it is better to work the shaping one stitch in from the edge, in order to avoid making a step in your fabric, which is particularly noticeable when working long crochet stitches in thicker yarns, and can cause difficulties when making up your garment.

To increase a treble or double treble at each end of a row

Stitches are increased at either end of the row in exactly the same way as for double crochet or half trebles: work two stitches into the stitch after the turning chain at the beginning of the row: then work across the row until only two stitches remain, including the turning chain, then work two stitches into the next stitch; finally, work the last stitch into the turning chain of the previous row. You will have increased two extra stitches — one stitch at each end of the row within a one-stitch border.

To decrease one treble at each end of a row

1 Make 3 chain at beginning of row where stitch is to be decreased.

2 Miss the first stitch in the normal way. Wind the yarn round the hook and insert hook into next stitch.

3 Wind yarn round hook and draw through a loop.

4 Wind yarn round hook and draw it through first 2 loops on hook.

5 Wind yarn round hook and insert it into next stitch.

6 Wind yarn round hook and draw a loop through.

Continued : decreasing one treble at each end of a row

7 There are now 4 loops on the hook.

8 Wind yarn round hook and draw it through first 2 loops on hook. 3 loops remain.

9 Wind yarn round hook and draw it through last 3 loops on hook. 2 treble have been worked together to decrease 1 stitch.

10 Work 1 treble into each treble until 3 stitches remain unworked. Do not forget to count the turning chain as 1 stitch.

11 Work the next 2 trebles together in the same way as at beginning of row. 1 stitch decreased at end of row.

12 Work the last treble into the turning chain of previous row.

To decrease one double treble at each end of a row

1 Work 4 chain at beginning of row where stitch is to be decreased.

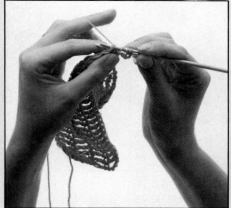

2 Miss the first stitch in the normal way. Wind the yarn twice round the hook and insert the hook into the next stitch.

3 Wind yarn round hook and draw through a loop. 4 loops on the hook.

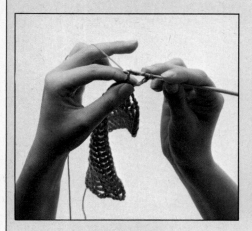

4 Wind yarn round hook and draw it through first 2 loops on hook.

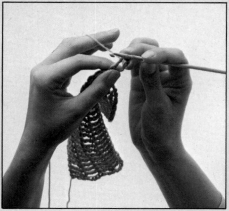

5 Wind yarn round hook and draw it through next 2 loops on hook. 2 loops remain.

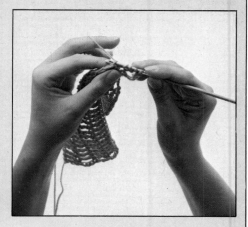

6 Wind yarn twice round hook and insert hook into next stitch.

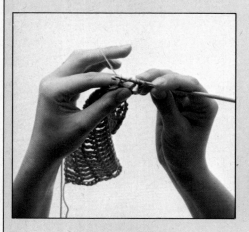

7 Wind yarn round hook and draw a loop through. 5 loops on the hook.

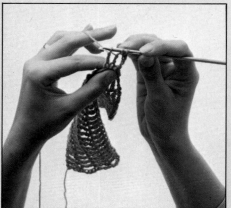

8 Repeat steps 4 and 5. 3 loops remain on hook.

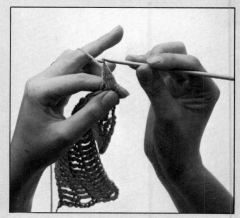

9 Wind yarn round hook and draw through all 3 loops on hook. 2 double treble have been worked together to decrease 1 stitch.

10 Work 1 double treble into each stitch across row until 3 stitches remain unworked. Do not forget to count the turning chain as 1 stitch.

11 Work the next 2 double treble together in the same way as at beginning of row. 1 stitch decreased.

12 Work the last double treble into the turning chain at the end of the row.

How to increase or decrease several stitches at each end of a row

It is possible to increase several stitches at each end of a row by working extra chain for each additional stitch required. When increasing stitches at the beginning of the row you will also need to add extra chain to allow for the turning chain, remembering that the number of turning chain will vary according to the stitch being worked. For example, if you are going to add an extra four double crochet you will need to make five chain

in all, whereas for four treble you will need to make six chain in all. The method for decreasing several stitches at the beginning or end of a row is the same for all crochet stitches. Work in slip stitch over the number of stitches to be decreased at the beginning of the row, then work a slip stitch into the next stitch and make the correct number of turning chain before working across the row in the normal way. To decrease several stitches

at the end of the row simply leave the required number of stitches unworked, remembering to always count the turning chain as one stitch, then turn and work back along the next row. Since the technique used for increasing several stitches at each end of the row is the same for all stitches, follow the working method given for double crochet but substitute the correct number of turning chain for the stitch being used.

To increase several double crochet at each end of a row

1 Work the extra number of chain you require at the beginning of the row, e.g. 5 chain for 4 double crochet.

2 Work the first double crochet into the 3rd chain from the hook, then 1 double crochet into each extra chain.

3 Continue to work in double crochet across row until 2 stitches remain. This will include the turning chain.

4 Leave the working loop on a spare hook.

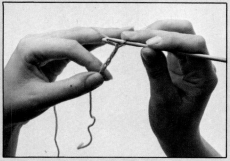

5 With a spare length of the correct yarn make a length of chain for the exact number of extra stitches, e.g. 4 chain for 4 double crochet.

6 Join this length of chain to the end of the row with a slip stitch. Fasten off yarn

7 Return to the working loop and work 1 double crochet into each of the last 2 stitches.

8 Work 1 double crochet into each of the extra chain. 4 double crochet increased at each end of row.

9 Work in double crochet across all stitches on the next row, including those just made.

Fluffy and flattering

Make something special for winter evenings. This glamorous mohair-look sweater, with batwing sleeves and bloused shape, has ribbons threaded through for added fashion interest.

Size
To fit 83 to 97cm bust.
Length to shoulder, 61cm.
Sleeve seam, 6.5cm.

Tension
9 stitches and 4 rows to 10cm worked over double treble on a 5.50mm hook.

Materials
Total of 325g of mohair-type yarn such as Wendy Sorbet
4.00mm crochet hook
5.50mm crochet hook
9m of 2.5cm-wide ribbon

Back and front (made in one piece)
☐ Begin at lower edge of front. Using 5.50mm hook make 42 chain loosely.

Shape front
☐ Work 1 double treble into 5th chain from hook, 1 double treble into same chain to increase 1 stitch, 1 double treble into each chain until 2 chain remain unworked, work 2 double treble into next chain to increase 1 stitch, 1 double treble into last chain. Turn. 41 double treble.
☐ Work 4 chain to count as first double treble, miss first double treble, 2 double treble into next double treble to increase 1 stitch, 1 double treble into each stitch until 2 double treble remain unworked, work 2 double treble into next stitch to increase 1 stitch, work last double treble into turning chain of previous row. Turn.
☐ Repeat the last row 14 times more.

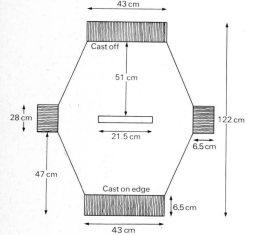

There will now be 71 double treble.

Work sleeves
☐ Place a marker at each end of last row to denote beginning of sleeves.
☐ Work 5 rows double treble without shaping.

Make neck opening
☐ Work over first 26 double treble, work 19 chain loosely, then miss next 19 double treble for neck opening, work 1 double treble into each stitch to end of row. Turn. Work over first 26 double treble, work 1 double treble into each of next 19 chain, work 1 double treble into each stitch to end of row. Turn. 71 double treble.
☐ Work 4 rows without shaping. Place a marker at each end of last row to denote end of sleeves.

Shape back
☐ Work 4 chain to count as first stitch, work next 2 double treble together to decrease 1 stitch, work 1 double treble into each stitch until 3 stitches remain unworked, work next 2 double treble together to decrease 1 stitch, work last double treble into turning chain of previous row. Turn.
☐ Repeat last row 15 times more. 39 double treble remain.
☐ Draw yarn through and fasten off.

To make back welt
☐ Using 4.00mm hook make 12 chain. Work 1 treble into 4th chain from hook, then 1 treble into each chain to end. Turn. 10 treble.
☐ Work 3 chain to count as first treble, work 1 treble into back loop only of each stitch to end. Turn.
☐ Repeat last row until welt is long enough to fit along lower edge.
☐ Draw yarn through and fasten off.

To make front welt
Work exactly as given for back welt.

To make cuffs
☐ Work as given for back welt until cuff fits along sleeve edge between markers.
☐ Work another cuff in the same way.

To make up
☐ Darn in all loose ends to wrong side using a blunt-ended wool needle.
☐ Thread ribbon through (here over and under every 3 stitches, every 3rd row), secure the ends.
☐ Using a flat seam sew welts to lower edge of back and front.
☐ Using a flat seam sew cuffs to sleeves between markers.
☐ Join underarm and side seams.

John Carter/accessories, Harvey Nichols

Step-by-step course – 8

* Working horizontal striped fabric
* Working vertical stripes — two methods
* Working diagonal stripes
* Start using abbreviations
* Pattern for a child's pinafore

Working horizontal stripes

Stripes are a good way to add extra colour or detail to a garment. They can be in sharp, contrasting colours or subtle shades. They can cross the fabric horizontally, vertically or diagonally. By varying the width of each stripe you can achieve a pleasing random effect.

Horizontal stripes are easy to work, especially if you use an even number of rows in each colour so that each colour begins and ends at the same edge. Our sample uses two colours, called A and B, and is worked in double crochet.

1 Make the desired number of chain with A. Work two rows with A, but do not complete the last stitch of the second row ; leave two loops on hook.

2 Loop B over hook and draw it through working loop. This completes the last stitch. Do not break off A.

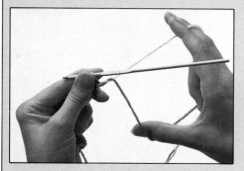

3 Turn the work. Twist B over and under A to hold A in place. Each colour is carried up the side of the work until it is needed again.

4 Work the next two rows in B. Do not complete the last stitch ; leave two loops on the hook.

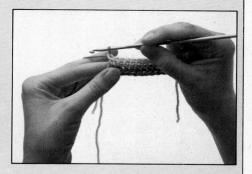

5 Pick up A and complete stitch in A.

6 Turn the work. Twist A over and under B to hold B in place.

7 Continue to work stripes in A and B, carrying yarns up the side until the desired number of stripes have been worked. Fasten off.

8 If you work an uneven number of rows in any colour you will need to break off the yarn and rejoin it at the other edge as shown.

Paul Williams

29

Working vertical stripes

This simple method is used where the stripes are only two or three stitches wide and the yarn is not too thick. The yarn is

The stranding method

carried across the back of the work. Our sample is made in double crochet and uses two colours, A and B.

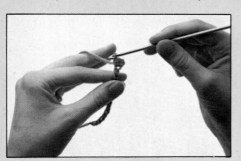

1 Make 19 chain with A; with A work one double crochet.

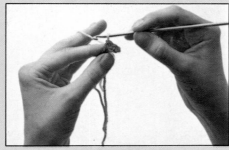

2 Change from A to B on next stitch by completing stitch with B. The first three stitches (turning chain counts as first stitch) will be in A.

3 Wind B round A. Keep A at back of work.

4 Work next two stitches in B.

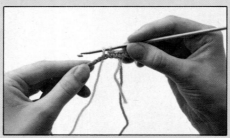

5 Insert hook into next stitch and draw through a loop. Leave B at back of work.

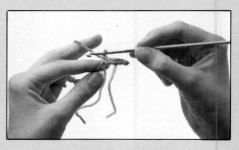

6 Pick up A. Carry A over B and complete stitch in A, taking care not to pull the stranded yarn too tight. There will be three stitches in B.

7 Continue to work three stitches in A and three in B across row in same way, but complete last stitch in B.

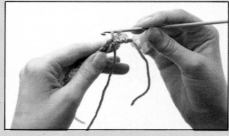

8 Turn and work first two stitches in B, insert hook into next stitch and draw through a loop. A will be at front of work.

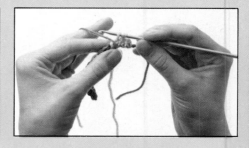

9 Bring B to front of work, then take A over B to back of work.

10 Complete stitch with A.

11 Continue to work in stripes across row, changing colours in same way each time, but complete last stitch in A.

12 Repeat these two rows until stripe pattern is complete. Fasten off.

The weaving method

The weaving method is used where the stripes are more than three stitches wide. The yarn being carried across the back of the work is linked in on top of one of the stitches in the stripe. The yarn is woven neatly into the back of the fabric.

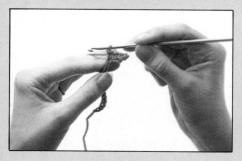

1 Work 21 chain in A, and work first three double crochet in A.

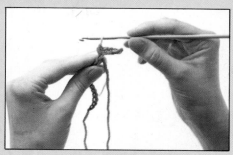

2 Change from A to B on next stitch by completing stitch with B. The first five stitches (including turning chain) will be in A.

3 Wind B round A. Keep A at back of work.

4 Work next two stitches in B. As you work the third stitch in B, hold A against the top edge of the row and crochet over it with the next stitch, taking care not to pull the stranded yarn too tight.

5 Keeping A at the back, work two more stitches in B, changing to A on the second stitch. Five stitches have now been worked in A and five in B.

6 Continue to work five stitches in A and five in B across row in same way, linking in the colour being woven on the third stitch of every stripe, but complete last stitch in B.

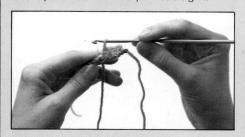

7 Turn and work the first four stitches in B, remembering to count the turning chain as the first stitch, and noting that A will be at front of work.

8 Insert hook into next stitch and draw through a loop.

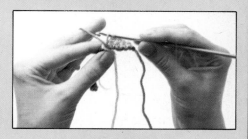

9 Bring B to front of work, then take A to back of work.

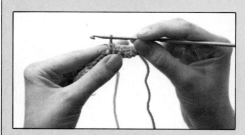

10 Complete stitch with A.

11 Continue to work in stripes across row, changing and linking in colours in the same way each time, but complete last stitch in A.

12 Repeat these two rows until stripe pattern is complete. Fasten off.

Paul Williams

Working diagonal stripes

These are worked in exactly the same way as vertical stripes, except that one stitch on each stripe is moved either to the right or to the left on every row to slant the stitches diagonally from right to left or left to right.

Strand the yarn across the back of the work and change the colours as needed in the same way as when working vertical stripes.

Start using abbreviations

Crochet has its own technical terms and a special language – a kind of shorthand – for describing instructions in a clear, concise way. Without this shorthand, the instructions for any but the simplest crochet are far too long and tedious to follow.

The abbreviations given here are for simple techniques that you already know: gradually these and other crochet notation will be introduced into patterns in the courses. As you become more practised at your crochet, you will find following the abbreviations becomes quite easy and automatic.

ch	=	chain
dc	=	double crochet
htr	=	half treble
tr	=	treble
dtr	=	double treble
tr tr	=	triple treble
st(s)	=	stitch(es)

Playtime pinny

What more could a small girl want? This practical pinafore dress is just the thing for a winter day's play. She will wear it time and again over jumpers, polo tops and blouses.

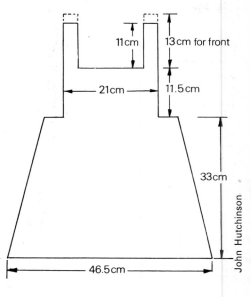

11cm

13cm for front

21cm

11.5cm

33cm

46.5cm

Size
To fit chest, 61cm.
Length, 56cm.

Tension
16sts and 14 rows to 10cm over htr on 4.00mm hook.

Materials
2 x 50g balls of Patons Fiona in main shade A, 1 ball each of contrasting colours B, C and D
4.00mm crochet hook
Waist length of elastic 15mm wide
2 buttons

Back

Using 4.00mm hook and B, make 74ch.

Base row Into 3rd ch from hook work 1htr, 1htr into each ch to end, joining in C on last htr. Turn.

Next row Using C, work 2ch to count as 1htr, 1htr into each htr to end, joining in A on last htr. Turn.

Continuing in htr, joining in colours as before, proceed as follows:

1st row Work with A.

2nd to 4th rows Work 2B, *3D, 3B, repeat from * to last 5sts, 3D, 2B.

5th row Work with A, but decrease 1htr at each end of row.

6th row Work with C.

7th row Work with B.

Working with A only, decrease 1htr at each end of 12th and every following 5th row until 57htr remain. Work 4 rows straight. Draw yarn through and fasten off.

Next row Miss first 12sts, join B to next st, 2ch, 1htr into each of next 32sts. Turn. Proceed on these 33sts as follows:

Next 3 rows Work 3B, *3D, 3B, repeat from * to end.

Work 1 row each in A, C, B and A.

Next 3 rows Work 3C, *3B, 3C, repeat from * to end.

Work 1 row each in A, D and B.

Next row Using C, work 2ch, 1htr into each of next 6htr. Turn.

Continue on these 7htr for strap, working in stripes of 1 row D, 1 row B and 1 row C until strap measures 11cm. Draw yarn through and fasten off.

Miss centre 19htr, join C to next htr, 2ch, 1htr into each of next 6htr. Continue on these 7htr to match first strap.

Front

Work as given for back, but make straps 13cm long instead of 11cm.

To make up

Sew in ends. Press lightly under a damp cloth with a warm iron. Using a flat seam, join the side seams.

Using B and with right side facing work a row of dc round outer edge of bib and straps.

Work herringbone casing over elastic on wrong side at waist. Sew 1 button to top of each back strap and use holes between htr on front straps to fasten.

Kim Sayer/Top by John Lewis

Step-by-step course – 9

*Working with separate balls
  of yarn
*Working longer stitches
*Pattern for a shawl

A tremendous variety of shapes and patterns can be achieved in crochet by using different colours. The possibilities include motifs repeated at regular intervals across your fabric, large motifs such as diamonds or rectangles, blocks of colours worked in a random pattern and a variety of colours to produce a patchwork effect.

Working with separate balls of yarn

Where the motif being worked is small and is repeated several times at regular intervals across the fabric, the yarn can be carried across the back of the work in the same way as for vertical stripes. Large motifs or patchwork patterns, however, should be worked using separate balls of yarn for each colour. This avoids wasting unnecessary lengths of yarn.

The separate balls can be wound on to a shaped piece of card, which acts rather like a bobbin and helps to prevent the different colours from becoming tangled. Our sample shows the technique used in wide stripes of double crochet and uses two colours, called A and B.

1 Make 31 chain with A and work 30 double crochet into chain. Turn.

2 Work first nine double crochet with A.

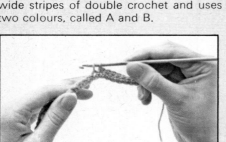

3 Insert hook into next stitch and draw a loop through.

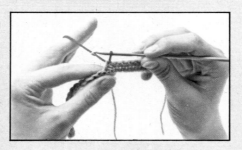

4 Draw next colour through working loop to complete stitch.

5 Wind B round A at back of work, passing B under and then over A. This winding of one yarn round the other prevents a gap where the stripes or shapes meet.

6 Work next nine double crochet in B, then change from B to second ball of A, repeating steps 3 and 4.

7 Repeat step 5 winding A round B.

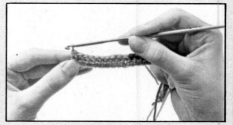

8 Work the last ten double crochet in A.

continued

Continued : working with separate balls of yarn

9 Turn and work first nine stitches in A. The wrong side of the work will be facing.

10 Insert hook into next stitch and draw a loop through.

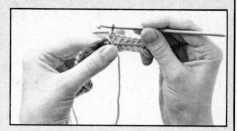

11 Bring A to front of work, take B to back of work and complete stitch with B.

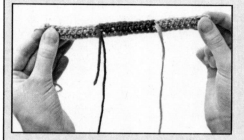

12 Continue to change colours at beginning of each stripe across the row in the same way, keeping the yarn not in use at the back of the work each time.

13 Work at least ten rows in this way so that you are familiar with the working method and can cope with both colours easily.

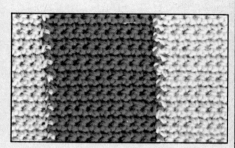

14 Sample showing the wrong side of the fabric.

Working longer stitches

Double crochet is really the ideal stitch for working motifs into a fabric. Because it is a shallow stitch, you can easily achieve a sloping edge on a motif ; whereas with deeper stitches, changes of colour made on a diagonal will produce a stepped effect. In working rectangles or squares, however, you can use treble or even deeper stitches effectively.

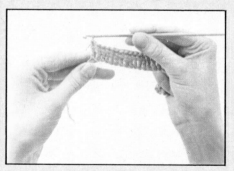

1 When working longer stitches such as double treble, work 31 chain, then work 28 double treble.

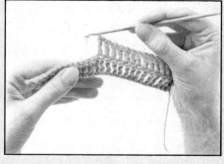

2 On the second row, work across the first 13 double treble (14 double treble including turning chain).

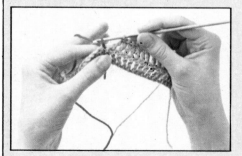

3 Insert hook into next stitch and work chain with next colour, to stand as next stitch (i.e. four for double treble).

4 You will now have two loops on the hook, one in each of the two colours.

5 Draw loop at top of chain through loop of first colour. Continue to the end of the row.

Paul Williams

Soft, muted shawl

Make this beautiful, soft shawl in muted shades as big as you fancy. Just work from the point upwards and finish when you like.

Size
Length at centre, 92cm.

Materials
Total of 350g of a mohair-type yarn such as Wendy Monaco
This shawl took 3 x 50g balls in each of colours grey-green and pink, 2 balls in cream.
5.00mm crochet hook.

Tension
11 double treble and 4¼ rows to 10cm.

To make shawl

Using green, make 5ch.
Base row Work 2dtr into 5th ch from hook. Turn.
Next row 4ch to count as first dtr, work 1dtr into first dtr – so increasing 1dtr, 1dtr into next dtr, 2dtr into the turning ch of previous row. Turn. 5dtr.
Next row 4ch, 2dtr into first dtr, 2dtr into each dtr to end. Turn. 9dtr.
Next row 4ch, 1dtr into first dtr, 2dtr into next dtr, work 1dtr into each dtr to within last 2dtr, work 2dtr into each of last 2dtr – so increasing 2dtr at each end of the row. Turn.
☐ Repeat the last row twice more, but join in pink on last dtr. 21dtr. Cut off green.
☐ Continuing to increase 2dtr at each end of every row, work in colour sections as follows:
Next row Work over first 9dtr, joining on cream on the 9th of these dtr (so having 11dtr worked in pink); with cream work to end of row.
Work 3 more rows using pink and cream. Cut off yarns.
Work 4 rows using green and pink. Cut off yarns.
Work 4 rows using cream and green. Cut off yarns.
Work 4 rows using pink and cream. Cut off yarns.
Work 4 rows using green and pink. Cut off yarns.
Repeat the last 12 rows once more. Fasten off.

Gary Warren/accessories Harrods

Step-by-step course – 10

*Making geometric patterns working from a chart
*Pattern for a waistcoat

Making geometric patterns working from a chart

More complicated patterns are sometimes worked from a chart, which shows the motif or pattern on graph paper. This method of representing the motif eliminates the need for lengthy row-by-row instructions. The charts are really quite clear and easy to follow, so do not be deterred by their seeming complexity.

Each square on the graph represents one stitch, and each horizontal line represents one row. The motif as represented on the graph will not be in proportion, since a square will not be the same width or depth as a stitch, and so the chart should be used as a plan only.

Begin reading the chart from the bottom right-hand corner, so that the first row is read from right to left. This will be the right side of the work; the second row, which is worked on the wrong side, will be read from left to right.

Where a motif is to be repeated a number of times during the course of a row, the chart will show only one complete pattern repeat, plus the stitches to be worked at each end of the row. The stitches within the pattern repeat should be repeated as many times as stated in the instructions, followed by the stitches to be worked at the end of the row. These end stitches will be the first stitches of the following row. Our sample is worked in two colours, coded A and B, in double crochet. A is represented by an X on the chart and B by a blank square. Carry the yarn not in use across the back of the work.

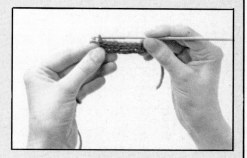

1 Make 11 chain with A; begin at bottom right-hand corner of chart and work two rows in A. These will be rows one and two on the chart.

2 Join on B ready for next row.

3 With right side of the work facing, work row three of chart from right to left.

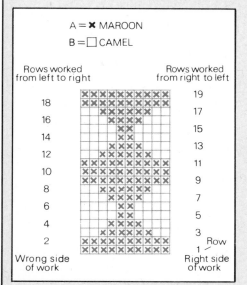

A = ✖ MAROON
B = ☐ CAMEL

Rows worked from left to right / Rows worked from right to left

Wrong side of work / Right side of work

4 Turn. With wrong side of the work facing, work row four of chart from left to right.

5 Continue to work each row in same way until motif is complete.

37

Home-spun waistcoat

Try out your own colour combinations and make this delightful patchwork-look waistcoat. A rich blend of colours gives it a really warm, home-spun look.

Gary Warren/accessories Harrods

Sizes
To fit 83/87cm bust.
Length at centre back, 46cm.

Materials
Total of 250g of double knitting and Aran yarn such as Sirdar Superwash Wool Double Knitting and Sirdar Sherpa
This garment took 3 x 25g balls of double knitting yarn in rust and brick and 1 ball in camel ; also 2 x 50g balls of Aran yarn in brown tweed
3.50mm crochet hook
Five buttons

Tension
17 treble and 9 rows to 10cm.

Back
Using rust, make 61ch.
☐ **Base row** 1tr into 4th ch from hook, 1tr into each ch to end. Turn. 59tr. Working in tr throughout proceed as follows :
☐ Beginning with row 2 on chart, work patchwork design until row 11 has been worked. Work 2tr into first and last tr on next row — so increasing 1tr at each end of the row. Increase 1 tr at each end of the following 4 alternate rows. 69tr. Fasten off.
Shape armholes
Next row Join brown to 6th tr from side edge and work 3ch to count as first tr ; work to within last 5 tr. Turn. 59tr.
☐ Continuing to follow the chart, work the first 2 tr and the last 2 tr together on the next row — so decreasing 1 tr at each end of the row. Decrease 1tr at each end of next 7 rows. 43tr. Work 9 rows straight. Fasten off.

Right front
Using rust, make 4ch.
Base row Work 2tr into 4th ch from hook. Turn. 3tr.
Beginning with row 2 on chart, work patchwork design shaping as follows :
☐ Increase 2tr at each end of next 3 rows. 15tr. Now increase 2tr at end of next row and at this same edge on following row. 19tr.
Next row Work to end increasing 2tr at end of row ; do not turn work but make 11ch for side edge extension. Turn.
Next row 1tr into 4th ch from hook, 1tr into each ch and tr to end. Turn. 30tr.
☐ Work straight until row 18 has been worked. Increase 1tr at end of next row

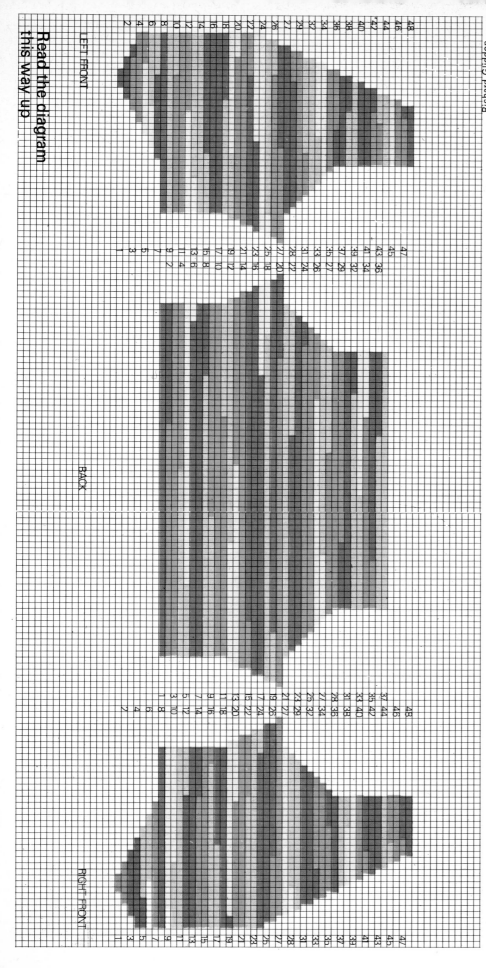

Richard Gliddon

and on the following 2 alternate rows. 33tr. Work 1 row straight.

Shape front edge

Continuing to increase 1tr at side edge, decrease 1tr at the beginning of the next and following alternate row. 33tr. Fasten off.

Shape armhole

Next row Join camel to 6th tr from side edge; work 3ch to count as first tr, work to end. Turn.

☐ Continuing to shape front edge on every alternate row, decrease 1 tr at armhole edge on next 8 rows. 16tr. Keeping armhole edge straight continue to shape front edge until 10tr remain. Work 1 row. Fasten off.

Left front

Work as given for right front, reversing shaping and working side edge extension thus: At the end of row 7 make 9ch using a separate ball of rust; fasten off and lay aside. Work row 8 to end of row, then work across the 9ch, so making 30tr.

The border

Join shoulder and side seams using a flat seam. With right side facing, join on brown and work a row of dc evenly all round outer edge, working 2dc into each st at front points and finishing by working a slip stitch into the first dc. Continuing to work 2dc into 2dc at points, work one round in rust, then one round in cream, making 5 evenly spaced buttonloops on the right front by working 2ch and missing 2dc. Next, work one round in brick working 2dc into each button loop, and one round in brown. Fasten off.

Armhole borders

Following the colour sequence as given for the border, work 5 rows of dc evenly all round armhole.

To make up

Press work using a warm iron over a damp cloth. Sew on the buttons.

Step-by-step course – 11

*Making a tubular fabric
*Two textured stitches
*Pattern for a striped bolster
*Pattern for a child's top

Making a tubular fabric

You've already learned to work in rounds, increasing on each round to make a flat motif. If you work in rounds without increasing, you can create a seamless tubular fabric of any width you like, which can be used to make a variety of garments, toys and household items, such as the multi-coloured bolster featured in this week's course. The tube is worked on to a basic circle, which should be the same size as the circumference of the article to be made.

Since the right side of the fabric will always be facing you, the stitches appear quite different from the way they look when worked in rows. However, if the work is divided at a given point, such as for the armhole shaping on a sweater, and then completed in rows, you must turn the work at the end of each round so that the stitches will always look the same throughout.

Try our sample using a double knitting yarn and 4.50mm hook.

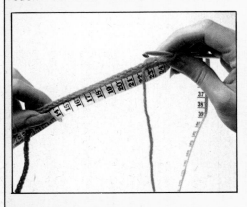

1 Make 45 chain. The length of chain should correspond exactly to the circumference of the circle to be made. Thus, if you were making a child's jersey measuring 60cm around the chest, you would need to begin by making a chain 60cm long. There is no need to add extra chain for turning.

2 Hold the hook in your right hand. Bring the free end of chain forward and up to the hook. Insert the hook into the first chain made. This prevents the chain from becoming twisted.

3 Wind the yarn over and round the hook from back to front and draw it through both loops on the hook to make a slip stitch.

4 Begin the round with the correct number of chain for the stitch being worked – in this case 3 chain for a treble. Hold the ring to the left of the hook and work 1 treble into the first chain to the left of these first 3 chain.

5 Work 1 treble into each following chain all the way round the circle so that you are working in a clockwise direction.

6 Join the last treble of the round to the 3rd of the first 3 chain – worked at the beginning of the round – with a slip stitch to complete the 1st round.

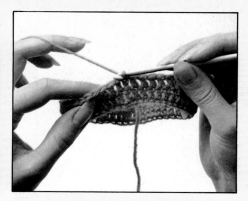

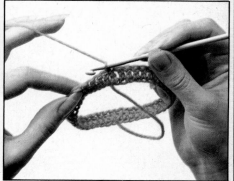

7 Begin the 2nd round by making 3 chain. Miss the first treble, which is the treble at the base of the first 3 chain. Now work 1 treble into the next treble.

8 Work 1 treble into each treble all the way round the circle and join the last treble to the top of the first 3 chain as before. By working continuously round the circle in this way you will always have the right side of the fabric facing you.

9 Where the fabric is to be divided at a given point the work must be turned at the end of each round. Work steps 1 to 6 as before. Do not continue to work round the circle, but turn the work so that the wrong side, or inside, of the tube is facing you.

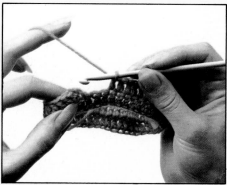

10 Now make 3 chain. The last stitch of the last round will now become the first stitch.

11 Now continue to work the next round as before, working in the same direction.

12 Continue to work as many rounds as required, remembering to join with a slip stitch and to turn the work at the end of each round until the section is completed.

Paul Williams

Two textured stitches

Here are two simple textured stitches for you to try. Both are worked in half trebles to give a firm, close fabric. You can make the samples in a double knitting yarn using a 4.50mm hook, or try using different yarns and hook sizes to see the varied effects which can be achieved with the same stitch.

Large granite stitch

This stitch should be worked over a number of chain divisible by two, with two extra for the turning chain.

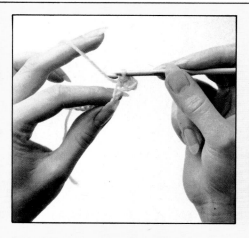

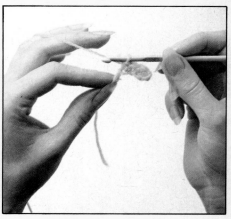

1 Make 22 chain and work 2 half treble into the 3rd chain from the hook. The first chain will count as the first htr of the row.

2 Miss the next chain and work two half treble into the next chain.

continued

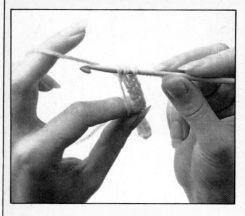 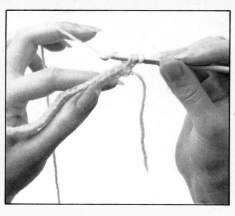 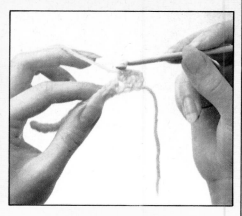

3 Repeat step 2 along the chain until 1 chain only remains unworked. Now work 1 half treble into this chain.

4 Turn the work. Make 2 chain to count as the first half treble. Now work 1 half treble between the first stitch at the edge of the work and the first half treble group. This will count as the first half treble group of the 2nd row.

5 Now work 2 half treble between the 2nd and 3rd half treble groups of the previous row.

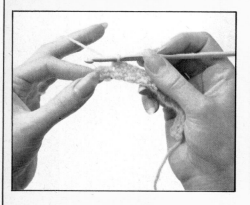 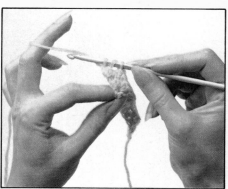 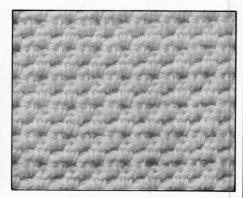

6 Continue to work in the same way as in step 5 between each half treble group of the previous row until the last half treble group has been reached.

7 Now work 1 half treble into the top of the 2 chain at the end of the row, to complete the 2nd row of the pattern.

8 Repeat steps 4 to 7 for every row, always working the first group as in step 4 and the last half treble into each turning chain of the previous row.

Crossed half trebles

This stitch makes use of a simple technique to produce a firm, thick fabric. The pattern is worked over a number of chain divisible by 2 plus 2 extra chain for the turning.

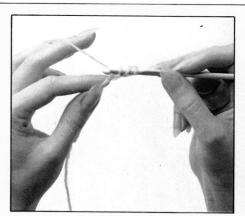 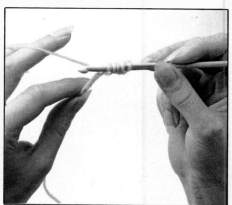

1 Make 22 chain for the base of the pattern. Wind yarn round the hook and insert it into 4th chain from hook. Wind yarn round hook again and draw through a loop so that there are 3 loops on the hook.

2 Wind yarn round hook again and insert it into the next chain. Wind yarn round the hook and draw a loop through once more. There are now 5 loops on the hook.

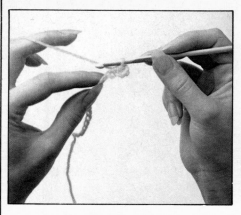

3 Wind the yarn round the hook and draw it through all 5 loops on the hook. You have now made a cluster group over 2 chain.

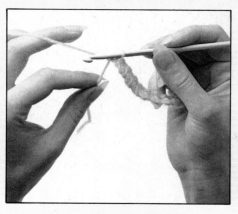

4 Now work one chain and then work another cluster group in the same way as before over the next 2 chain. Continue to work 1 cluster group over every 2 chain until only one chain remains unworked. Work 1 chain and then one half treble into the last chain.

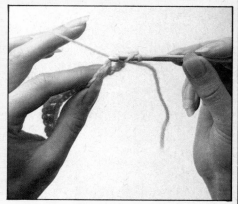

5 Turn the work and make 3 chain which will count as the first half treble and 1 chain space. Wind the yarn round the hook and insert the hook into the first 1 chain space of the previous row. Now wind yarn round hook and draw through a loop.

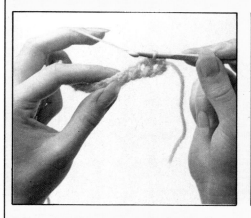

6 Complete the cluster group by working as before into the next 1 chain space in the previous row.

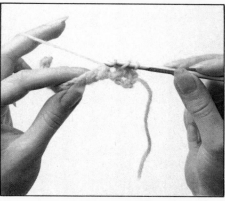

7 Make 1 chain. Now wind yarn round the hook and insert the hook into same space as the last stitch just worked. Wind yarn round the hook and draw through a loop.

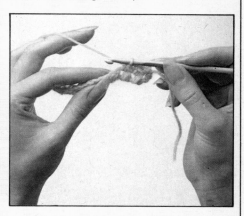

8 Wind yarn round hook and insert it into the next 1 chain space. Wind yarn round hook and draw through a loop.

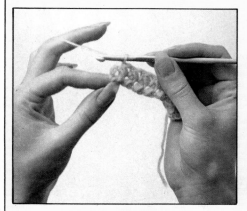

9 Repeat steps 7 and 8 across the row, beginning to work each group in the same space as the last stitch just worked until only the turning chain remains unworked in the previous row.

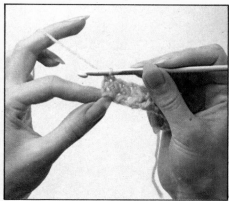

10 Make 1 chain. Now work 1 half treble into the top of the turning chain of the previous row to complete the 2nd row.

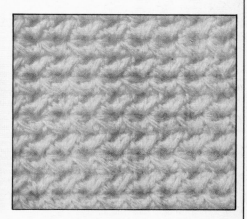

11 The 2nd row forms the pattern for this stitch. Repeat it for at least 10 rows to obtain the full effect of this stitch.

A bright way with stripes

You'll enjoy making this big bolster cover with its bright-coloured stripes, worked in rounds. It's a simple way to add a decorative — and practical — furnishing to your home.

Size
The cover measures 25.5cm in diameter x 77.5cm long.
The circles at the ends of the bolster are 25.5cm in diameter.

Materials
Total of 1000g of Aran yarn such as Lister/Lee Target Aran
Our cover took 350g of green, called A in instructions, 250g of yellow (B) and 400g of rust (C)
5.00mm crochet hook
Bolster to fit. The bolster should be 2.5cm larger in diameter and approx. 5cm longer than the cover to ensure a smooth fit.

Tension
18 sts and 20 rounds to 13cm worked over htr on a 5.00mm hook.

To make first circle
Work circle in stripes of 2 rounds A, 2 rounds B and 2 rounds C throughout. Using A, make 6ch, join into a circle with a ss.
1st round Make 2ch to count as first htr, now work 10htr into circle, join with a ss to 2nd of first 2 ch. 11 sts.
2nd round 2 ch to count as first htr, 1htr into first st ; now work 2htr in to each st round circle, join with a ss to 2nd of first 2ch. 22 sts.
3rd round 2ch, *1htr into each of next 2 sts, 2htr into next st, rep from * 6 times more, 1htr into st at base of 2ch ; join with a ss to 2nd of first 2ch. 30 sts.
4th round 2ch, 1htr into each of next 2 sts, 2htr into next st, *1htr into each of next 3 sts, 2htr into next st, rep from * 5 times more, 1htr into each of next 2 sts, join with a ss to 2nd of first 2ch. 37 sts.

5th round 2ch, 1htr into each of next 2 sts, 2htr into next st, *1htr into each of next 4 sts, 2htr into next st, rep from * 5 times more, 1htr into each of next 3 sts ; join with a ss to 2nd of first 2ch. 44 sts.
6th round 2ch, 1htr into each of next 2 sts, 2htr into next st, *1htr into each of next 5 sts, 2htr into next st, rep from * 5 times more, 1htr into each of next 4 sts, join with a ss to 2nd of first 2ch. 51 sts. Continue to increase 7 sts in this way on every round, beginning each round as given for 6th round and working one more st between increases at the end of each subsequent round, until 17 rounds in all have been worked and there are 128 sts. Do not break off yarn.

To make bolster
Continue to work in rounds making a tube for main part of bolster.
Next round 2ch, miss first st, 1htr into each st all the way round the circle. Join last htr to top of first 2ch with a ss. 127 sts.

Work square pattern
Use separate balls of yarn for each block of colour, twisting the yarns at the back of the work when changing colours. You will need to turn the work at the end of each round, after joining with a ss, so that the different colours are in the correct position when working the following round.
1st round 2ch, miss first st, work 18 sts A, *3 sts B, 18 sts C, 3 sts B, 18 sts A, repeat from * once more. Now work 3 sts B, 18 sts C and 3 sts B. Join last htr to 2nd of first 2ch with a ss. Turn. There are 6 large blocks with a small block of B between each.
Work 19 more rounds in this way, keeping colour pattern correct, and turning work at the end of each round. Cut off additional balls of yarn. Turn work at the end of the last round so that you will be working the striped pattern in the correct direction.
Now continue to work continuous rounds in stripes of 2 rounds B, 8 rounds A, 2 rounds B, 8 rounds C and 2 rounds B. Repeat square pattern once more, but working C instead of A and vice versa. Turn work once more so that you are working in the right direction and work stripe pattern once more. Work 8 rounds in A. Draw yarn through and fasten off. Make a 2nd circle as given for first until 17 rounds in all have been worked, but working A in place of C and vice versa. Fasten off.

To make up
Darn all loose ends of yarn to WS of work. Insert bolster in cover. With RS of 2nd

Bolster
25·5 cm diameter

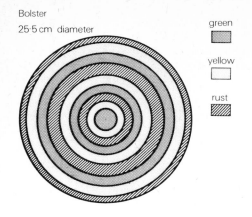

green

yellow

rust

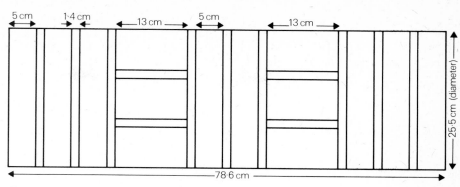

5 cm 1·4 cm 13 cm 5 cm 13 cm

25·5 cm (diameter)

78·6 cm

circle facing, rejoin A to a half treble on 17th round. Working through both thicknesses, join circle to top edge of bolster with dc. Work a round of dc in C through last round of first circle and first row of tube in the same way at other end.

To make your own filling
You will need a piece of foam rubber measuring approximately 2.5cm thick by 2.5m long by 78cm wide. Roll it into a tube so that it is approximately 28cm in diameter – that is, 2.5cm larger

than the cover. Make a tube from a sheet of unbleached calico 85cm by 83cm to cover the foam rubber, with a circle at each end 31cm in diameter to complete the tube. (These measurements give you 1.5cm seam allowances.)

Rounds for applause

For playtime – or anytime – a child needs clothes with lots of 'give'. This comfortable sweater, crocheted in rounds, is sure to be an all-time favourite.

Size
To fit 51[56:61:66]cm chest.
Length, 34.5[42.5:46.5:52]cm.
Sleeve seam, 32.5[35:37.5:40]cm.
Note the instructions for larger sizes are given in square brackets [] ; where there is only one set of figures it applies to all sizes.

Materials
Total of 350[450:500:550]g of double knitting yarn such as Patons Behive double knitting 4.00mm crochet hook

Tension
17htr and 12 rows to 10cm worked on a 4.00mm hook.

Back and front (worked in a tubular fabric to armhole).
Make 96[104:112:120]ch. Join the last ch to the first with a ss, taking care not to twist the ch.
Base row 2ch to count as first htr, miss 1ch, work 1htr into each ch to end of round. Join with a ss to first ch. Turn.
1st round 2ch, miss first htr, work 1htr into each st to end of round. Join with a ss to first ch. Turn. Rep the 1st round throughout, turning the work at the end of each round until 26[30:32:36] rows in all have been worked. You can adjust the length at this point if necessary.

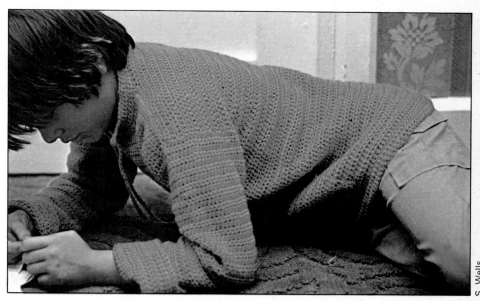

S. Wells

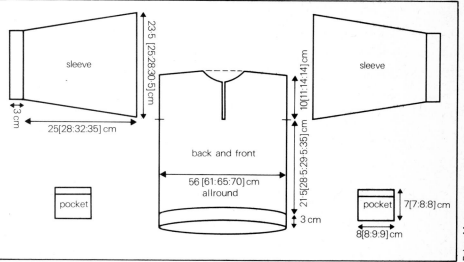

sleeve

23·5 [25:28:30·5] cm

25[28:32:35] cm

3 cm

sleeve

10[11:14:14] cm

back and front

56 [61:65:70] cm
allround

21·5[28·5:29·5:35] cm

3 cm

pocket

pocket 7[7:8:8] cm

8[8:9:9] cm

Brian Mayor

16[18 :20 :20]htr remain, ending at neck edge.

Shape shoulder
Work across first 8[9 :10 :10]htr, turn and leave remaining 8[9 :10 :10] sts unworked.
Work 1 more row. Draw yarn through and fasten off.
With right side of front facing, rejoin yarn at front neck opening. Complete the second half of front to match the first, reversing the shaping so that armhole and neck are worked in the correct position on this side.

Welt
Rejoin yarn to lower edge of body at side edge.
Next round 1ch, work 1dc into each st all round lower edge of sweater. Join with a ss to first ch. Turn.
Rep this round 4 times more. Draw yarn through.
Fasten off.

Sleeves
Join shoulder seams on wrong side of work. With right side of work facing, rejoin yarn to underarm. Work 40[44 :48 :52] htr evenly all round armhole ; join last htr to first with a ss, so forming a circle.
Continue in tubular fabric as given for body, decreasing one st at each end of every following 6th[7th :8th :8th] round until 30[34 :38 :42] sts remain.
Continue without shaping until 36[40 :42 :46] rounds an all have been worked.
You can adjust length here if necessary. Do not cut off yarn.

Cuff
Continue in rounds as before, work 4 rounds in dc. Draw yarn through and fasten off.

Neckband
With right side of front facing, rejoin yarn to right front at neck edge. Work 44[46 :48 :50]dc evenly round neck edge, ending at left front neck edge. Turn.
Work 4[4 :5 :5] rows in dc on these sts.
Do not fasten off. Continue to work 1 row in dc down one side of front opening, up other side and round neck edge again.
Fasten off.

Pockets (make 2)
Make 14[14 :16 :16]ch. Work 8[8 :10 :10] rows in htr, then 3 rows in dc on these sts.
Fasten off.

To make up
Darn all loose ends in on wrong side of work. Press lightly under a damp cloth with a warm iron. Sew pockets to front. With double thickness of yarn make a chain 85[85 :90 :90]cm long. Using spaces between stitches at neck edge, lace cord up front opening as shown. Turn back cuff to required depth.

Divide for back
Work across first 48[52 :56 :60] htr, turn. Continue to work in rows on these sts for back with 2 turning chain at the beginning of each row. Work 12[14 :16 :16] more rows.

Shape shoulders
*Ss across first 8[9 :10 :10] sts, continue in pattern across row until 8[9 :10 :10] sts remain unworked, turn and leave these sts for 2nd shoulder. Rep from * once more, then draw yarn through loop on hook and fasten off.

Work front and divide for front opening
Return to remaining sts. Rejoin yarn at armhole edge and pattern across first 24[26 :28 :30] sts, turn and complete this side first.
Work 7[9 :11 :13] rows.

Shape front neck
Pattern across first 20[20 :22 :24] sts, turn and leave remaining 4[6 :6 :6] sts unworked.
Decrease 1 htr at neck edge on next and every following row (by working 2htr together one st in from neck edge) until

S. Wells

Step-by-step course – 12

*Increasing within a row
*Decreasing within a row
*Pattern for a chevron-striped skirt

Sometimes you will need to increase or decrease within a row, instead of at the ends, in order to produce the shape required. On a skirt, for example, the fabric must be shaped smoothly from the waist over the hips. Increasing or decreasing within the row achieves this.

Another use for this kind of shaping is in making patterns, such as chevron stripes. By decreasing regularly at certain points you produce downward-pointing angles; by increasing regularly at intermediate points you produce upward-pointing angles, thus forming the familiar, wave-like pattern.

Increasing a stitch within a row

Increasing within a row is very simple: you just work two or more stitches into the stitch where the increase is required. It is a good idea to mark this stitch with a coloured thread, since you will probably have to increase again on subsequent rows above it. Our sample is worked in trebles, but the technique is the same for other stitches.

1 Make 14 chain and work two rows in treble. There will be 12 trebles in each row.

2 Work across the first four trebles of the next row: five trebles (counting the turning chain as one treble).

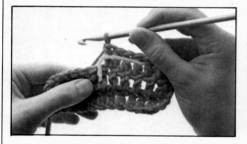

3 Work two trebles into next stitch. Place a marker in the increased stitch.

4 Work one treble into each treble to end of row. Turn.

5 Work across the first five trebles of the next row: six trebles (counting the turning chain as one treble).

6 Work two trebles into next stitch (the first of the two increased stitches).

7 Work one treble into each treble to end of row. Turn. Continue increasing in this way on the first of the increased stitches on the wrong side rows (this will be the second stitch on the right side rows). Note that the line of shaping produced in this way slants to the left on the right side of the fabric.

8 By increasing into the second of the two increased stitches on the wrong side (first of the increased stitches on the right side) you achieve a shaping that slants to the right. To keep the line of shaping vertical, increase in the first stitch and in the second on alternate rows.

Paul Williams

47

Decreasing within a row

The technique for decreasing within a row is essentially the same for each crochet stitch. Our sample is worked in treble, but you can adapt the method for other stitches using the detailed instructions for decreasing double crochet half trebles or double trebles at the end of a row.

1 Make 14 chain and work two rows in treble. There will be 12 trebles in each row.

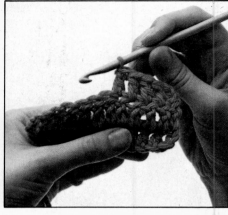

2 Work across the first four trebles of the next wrong side row : five trebles (counting the turning chain as one treble).

6 Repeat step 3 into the *next* stitch. Wind yarn round hook and draw through a loop. There should be four loops on the hook.

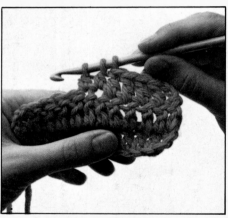

7 Repeat step 5. There will be three loops left on the hook this time.

8 Wind yarn round hook and draw through remaining three loops. One stitch has been decreased. Place a marker in the first stitch of the two you have worked together.

12 The line of decreases will slant to the left on the right side of the work.

13 To make the line of decreases slant to the right on the right side of the work, begin by repeating steps one to nine as before.

14 Work across four trebles of next row ; five trebles (counting the turning chain as one treble).

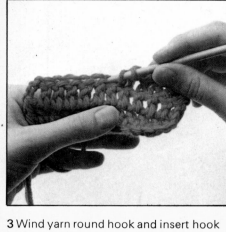

3 Wind yarn round hook and insert hook into next stitch.

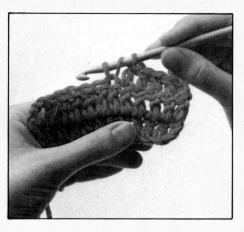

4 Wind yarn round hook and draw through a loop. There should be three loops on the hook.

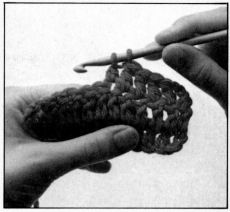

5 Wind yarn round hook and draw through first two loops on the hook. Two loops remain on the hook.

9 Work one treble into each treble to end of row. Turn.

10 Work across three trebles of next row : four trebles (counting the turning chain as one treble).

11 Work the next two trebles together as for previous row.
Work one treble into each treble to the end of the row.

15 Work the next two trebles together as before.

16 Work one treble into each treble to end of row.

17 Here the line of decreases slants to the right. To keep the line of shaping vertical decrease to the right and to the left on alternate rows.

Paul Williams

Chevron skirt

Flattering chevron stripes in four shades of brown and beige make a skirt you'll enjoy wearing time and time again. You'll also enjoy working the stripes and seeing their intriguing pattern emerge as you progressively increase and decrease the stitches.

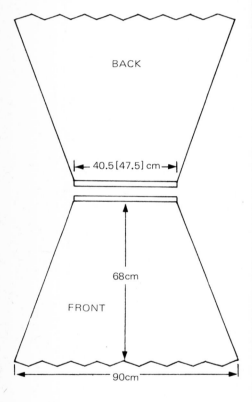

BACK

←—40.5 [47.5] cm—→

68cm

FRONT

90cm

Sizes
To fit 91-97[102-107]cm hips.
Length when hanging, 68cm.

Materials
Total of 450 [600] g of double
knitting yarn such as Pingouin
Confortable
This garment took 3[3] x 50g balls in
first colour, A
2[3] balls in 2nd colour, B
2[3] balls in 3rd colour, C
2[3] balls in 4th colour, D
4.00mm crochet hook
Waist length of 2.5cm wide elastic
18cm zip fastener

Tension
15tr and 7½ rows to 10cm over plain tr.
17tr to 10cm over chevron patt.

50

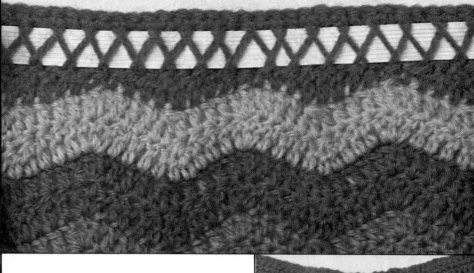

Back and front (alike)

Using A, make 148[172]ch.

Base row 1tr into 4th ch from hook, *1tr into each of next 10ch, work 3tr together over next 3ch, 1tr into each of next 10ch, 3tr into next ch, repeat from asterisk (*) to end, but finish last repeat 2tr into last ch instead of 3tr. Turn. 145[169]tr.

Next row 3ch to count as 1tr, 1tr into first tr, *1tr into each of next 10tr, work 3tr together, 1tr into each of next 10tr, 3tr into next tr, repeat from * to end, but finish last repeat 2tr into turning ch of previous row and join in B on last tr. Turn.

Repeat the last row, working 2 rows in each of B, C, D, A, B, C and D and join in A on last tr – so completing 16 rows from the beginning.

1st decrease row Using A, work 3ch, miss first tr, 1tr into each of next 10tr, *work 3tr together, 1tr into each of next 21tr, repeat from * to end, but finish last repeat 1tr into each of last 11tr. Turn.

Next row 3ch, 1tr into first tr, *1tr into each of next 9tr, work 3tr together, 1tr into each of next 9tr, 3tr into next tr, repeat from * to end, but finish last repeat 2tr into last tr, and join in B on last tr. Turn.

Using B, repeat the last row twice more, joining in C on last tr of second row.

2nd decrease row Using C, work 3ch, 1tr into each of next 9tr, *work 3tr together, 1tr into each of next 19tr, repeat from * to end, but finish last repeat 1tr into each of last 10tr. Turn.

Next row 3ch, 1tr into first tr, *1tr into each of next 8tr, work 3tr together, 1tr into each of next 8tr, 3tr into next tr, repeat from * to end, but finish last repeat 2tr into last tr, and join in D on last tr. Turn.

Using D, repeat the last row twice more, joining in A on last tr of second row.

3rd decrease row Using A, work 3ch, miss first tr, 1tr into each of next 8tr, *work 3tr together, 1tr into each of next 17tr, repeat from * to end, but finish last repeat 1tr into each of last 9tr. Turn.

Next row 3ch, 1tr into first tr, *1tr into each of next 7tr, work 3tr together, 1tr into each of next 7tr, 3tr into next tr, repeat from * to end, but finish last repeat 2tr into last tr, and join in B on last tr. Turn.

Continue in this way, working in stripe sequence and pattern as now set, decreasing on every 4th row, as before, until 61[71] tr remain.

Work 7 rows, so ending 2 rows in D, joining in A on last tr of 3rd row.

Next row Using A, work 1ch, miss first tr, *1dc into next tr, 1htr into each of next 2tr, 1 tr into each of next 3tr, 1htr into each of next 2tr, 1dc into next tr, repeat from * to end, finishing 1dc into last tr. Turn.

Work 4 rows in dc. Fasten off.

To make up

Do not press. Using a backstitch seam, join side seams leaving 18cm from top edge open. Sew in the zip fastener. Work herringbone casing over elastic on wrong side at waist. Press seams lightly with a warm iron over a damp cloth.

Step-by-step course – 13

Practical and fashionable, these scarves illustrate the versatility of crochet. Three different kinds of yarn and three different stitch patterns create three individual styles.

Silky scarf

Size
18cm wide by 184 cm long, excluding fringe.

Materials
  10 balls of Twilleys Lystwist (rayon yarn)
  1.75mm crochet hook

To make
Using 1.75mm hook make 57ch.
1st row 1tr into 4th ch from hook, 1tr into each of next 7ch, *1ch, miss next ch, 1tr into each of next 17ch, rep

from * once more, 1ch, miss next ch, 1tr into each of last 9ch. Turn.
2nd row 3ch to count as first tr, 1tr into each of next 7tr, *1ch, miss next tr, 1tr into next sp, 1ch, miss next tr, 1tr into each of next 15tr, rep from * once more, 1ch, miss next tr, 1tr into next sp, 1ch, miss next tr, 1tr into each of last 7tr, 1tr into the turning ch. Turn. Beg row 3, cont in patt working from chart until the 1st row of the 12th patt has been worked. Fasten off.

Fringe
Using three 45cm lengths of yarn tog knot fringe.

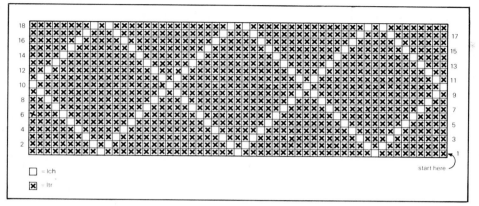

☐ = 1ch
☒ = 1tr

start here

To make a knotted fringe

Cut the yarn into the required lengths. For the long, silky scarf you will need strands 45cm long. Take three strands together at a time and knot fringe as follows.

Holding the right side of the edge to be fringed so that it is facing you, insert a crochet hook through the edge from back to front, fold the three strands in half and place the loop on the hook.

Pull the hook towards you, so pulling the loop through the fabric.

Slide the hook upwards, around the six strands, and draw the ends of yarn through the loop. Pull the knot up tightly.

Knot each fringe in the same way at regular intervals along the edge.

Mohair scarf
(See photo on page 52.)

Size
24cm wide by 224cm long.

Materials
  7 x 25g balls of Hayfield Gossamer
    (mohair yarn)
  4.00mm crochet hook

To make
Using 4.00mm hook make 46ch.
Base row 1tr tr into 8th ch from hook,
*1ch, miss next ch, 1tr tr into next ch,
rep from * to end.
Turn.
Patt row 6ch to count as first tr tr and
1ch, 1tr tr into next tr tr, *1ch, 1tr tr
into next tr tr, rep from * to end,
finishing 1ch, miss next ch, 1tr tr
into next ch.
Turn. 20sps.
Rep the patt row until work measures
222cm from beg.
Edging row *4ch, 1dc into next sp,
rep from * to end.
Fasten off.
Join yarn to base row and work edging
row along this edge.

Triangular scarf

Size
80cm wide by 48cm deep, measured at
widest parts.

Materials
  2 x 25g balls of Jaegar Faeriespun
    (2 ply yarn)
  2.00mm crochet hook

To make
Using 2.00mm hook make 6ch, join
with a ss to first ch to form a circle.
1st row 5ch to count as first dtr and 1ch,
work 1dtr, 1ch and 1dtr into circle.
Turn. 2sps.
2nd row 5ch, 1dtr into first sp, 1ch,
1dtr into same sp, 1ch, 1dtr into next sp,
1ch, 1dtr into same sp. Turn. 4sps.
3rd row 5ch, 1dtr, 1ch and 1dtr all into
first sp, (1ch, 1dtr into next sp)
3 times, 1ch, miss next ch, 1dtr into
next ch. Turn. 6sps.
4th row 5ch, 1dtr, 1ch and 1dtr all into
first sp, now work 1ch and 1dtr into
each sp to end, finishing 1ch, 1dtr
into last dtr. Turn.
Rep the last row until there are 88 sps.
Now work edging thus :
Next round Work 3dc into each sp along
the 3 sides and 6dc into each corner sp,
finishing ss into first dc.
Next round 3ch, work 5tr all into first dc,
*miss next 2dc, ss into next dc,
miss next 2dc, 6tr all into next dc,
rep from * all round, finishing ss into
top of the 3ch.
Fasten off.

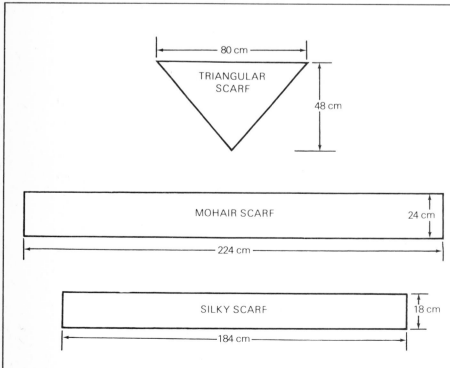

Step-by-step course – 14

Making a flat square motif

Many different motifs can be produced by working in rounds to create a flat shape, but possibly the best known and easiest to work is the granny square. The squares can be worked in either one or several colours and joined together to make a great variety of rugs, blankets, shawls and garments.

To make this sample use a 4.50mm hook and double knitting yarn.

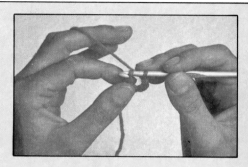

1 Make 8 chain and then loop the chain round to form a circle, inserting the hook from front to back into the first chain made.

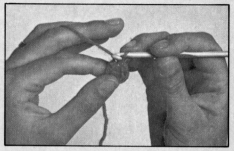

2 Wind the yarn round the hook and draw it through both the loops on the hook, so that the chain is joined together with a slip stitch.

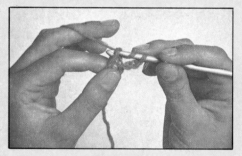

3 Work 3 chain, which will count as the first treble of the first round. Now wind the yarn round the hook and insert the hook from front to back through the centre of the circle – not into the chain stitch itself.

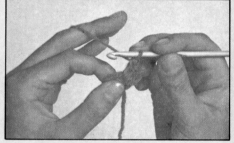

4 Complete this treble in the normal way and then work one more treble into the circle in the same way. There will now be 1 group of 3 treble, including the first 3 chain, worked into the circle.

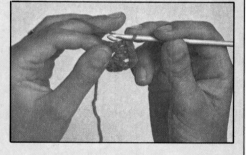

5 Make 2 chain. These 2 chain will be counted as the first corner of the square and will be called a 2 chain space. Now work 3 more treble into the centre of the circle as before.

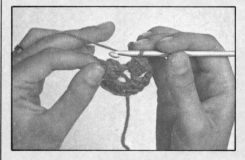

6 Repeat step 5 twice more, so that you will have 4 groups of 3 treble worked into the circle, and three 2 chain spaces. Work 2 chain for the last corner, and then insert the hook from front to back into the 3rd of the first 3 chain, worked at the beginning of the round.

7 Wind the yarn round the hook and draw it through both loops on the hook so that the beginning and end of the round are joined together with a slip stitch. This completes the first round of the square.

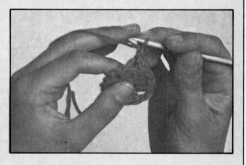

8 Continue to work round the square, without turning the work, so that the right side of the motif is always facing you. Unlike working in rows, there is a definite right and wrong side to the fabric when working in rounds. Begin the 2nd round by working 2 chain.

Frederick Mancini

continued

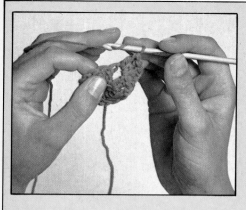

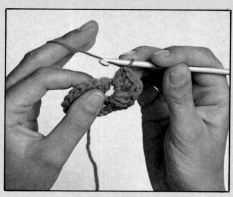

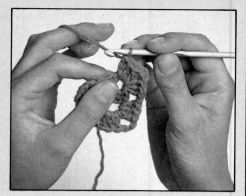

9 Work 3 treble into the next 2 chain space after the first block of trebles worked in the first round, inserting the hook from front to back under the 2 chain each time.

10 Make 2 chain and then work 3 treble into the same space as the 3 treble just worked. This will be the first corner group of the 2nd round. All the corners will be made in the same way on each round.

11 Make 1 chain and then work the next corner group as before into the next 2 chain space.

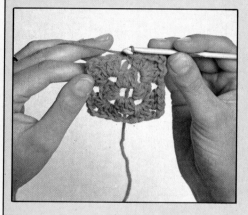

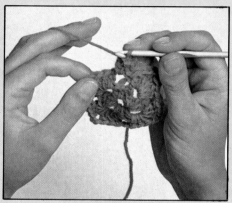

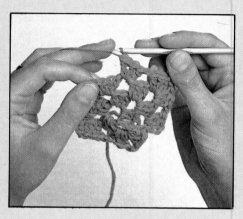

12 Complete the 3rd and 4th corners of the 2nd round in the same way. You will have now worked 4 corners in all with a 1 chain space between each corner. Join the end of the round to the beginning by working a slip stitch into the first of the 2 chain at the beginning of the round. The 2nd round has now been completed.

13 Work 3 chain to count as the first treble of the next round. Now work 2 treble into the first space after the slip stitch joining the previous round.

14 Work 1 chain and then work a corner group into the first corner space. Then work 1 chain, 1 group of 3 treble into the 1 chain space on the previous row, then 1 chain.

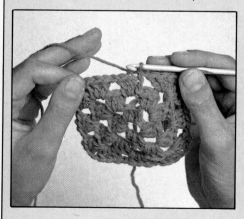

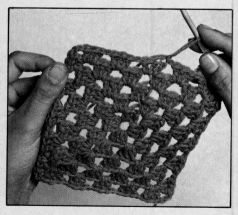

15 Complete the 3rd round in the same way, joining the last chain to the 3rd of the first 3 chain at the beginning of the round with a slip stitch.

16 The 4th round is worked in the same way, but with 2 groups of treble worked in each of the 1 chain spaces on each side of the square.

17 To make the sample bigger, continue to work as many rounds as you like for the size of motif required, working 1 more treble group on each side of the square on every subsequent round, with 1 chain between each group.

Frederick Mancini

Introducing a new colour in a square motif

Follow this method if you want to introduce a new colour into the work without it showing in the previous round.

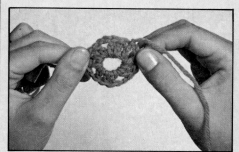

1 Complete the first round with the first colour. When you have worked the final slip stitch joining the beginning and the end of the round, draw the yarn through the last loop and fasten off. Cut off the yarn, leaving a length long enough to be darned into the back of the fabric when the motif has been completed.

2 Insert the hook into the centre of the next corner after the slip stitch that joined the ends of the last round together, and draw through a loop of the new colour. Remember to leave a length of yarn long enough to be darned in afterwards.

3 Work 1 chain with both ends of the yarn to hold it firmly in place. Now drop the free end of the yarn.

4 Work 2 more chain so that you have worked 3 chain in all, to count as the first treble of this round. Complete the round in the normal way with the new colour.

5 Change colour at the beginning of each round in the same way until the motif has been completed.

6 Darn all the loose ends in to the back of the fabric, taking care to sew each end into its own colour.

Sewing several motifs together

Use this method of joining motifs, such as granny squares, that have straight side edges.

1 Place two motifs together, right sides facing, so that the wrong side of each motif is on the outside. Pin them together along one side, about 1 round in from the edge.

2 For sewing the motifs together use a blunt-ended wool needle and the yarn used in the motif. If this is too thick, use a matching yarn in a finer ply. Begin at the right-hand edge of the square and oversew the two together, taking care not to pull the yarn too tightly.

3 Sew all the motifs together in the same way, sewing them first into horizontal strips and then sewing the strips together. By using this method, you will find it easier to get the seams to run straight.

Frederick Mancini

58

Giant cushions

These giant cushions are almost a substitute for sitting-room furniture. Make striking covers in bright-coloured stripes, or use more natural shades for a more subdued effect.

Multi-striped cushion

Size
Our cover has been made to fit a cushion pad measuring 91.5cm by 91.5cm square. It measures approximately 89cm by 89cm square, 2.5cm less than pad. Each square measures approximately 42cm by 42cm, excluding edging.

Materials
> 25 x 50g balls of Pingouin Sport in blue
> 5 balls in white
> 4 balls in each of red, green and yellow
> 4.00mm crochet hook
> A cushion pad 91.5cm by 91.5cm square

Tension
18 htr and 11 rows to 10cm on a 4.00mm hook.

Note To make the cover for a different-sized pad or for an existing cushion, measure the width of your cushion pad and make your cover 2.5cm less. This ensures a smooth, snug fit. For example, a cushion measuring 63.5cm by 63.5cm square will need a cover measuring 61cm by 61cm square. Allow 2.5cm all round for edging and subtract this figure from the original size so that area for remaining squares will be 56cm by 56cm square.
Each square will therefore measure approximately 28cm by 28cm.

To make the striped square
We quote the colours used in our cushion. You can, of course, use any colour combination you like, but remember that you will need more of 1 colour than the others to make the back.
Using 4.00mm hook and red make 10ch, join with a slip stitch to first ch to form a circle.
1st round Work 2ch to count as first htr, then work 15htr into circle; join the last htr to the top of first 2ch worked with a slip stitch. There are 16htr.
2nd round Work 2ch, which will count as first htr; work 2htr into same place as slip stitch – 1 corner formed, *1htr into each of next 3htr, 3htr all into next htr – corner formed, repeat from asterisk (*) twice more, then work 1htr into each of

next 3htr, join last htr worked to top of first 2ch with a slip stitch. Fasten off.
3rd round Join white to 2nd htr of one corner group, 2ch, now work 1htr, 1ch and 2htr all into same htr, *(1ch, miss next htr, 1htr into next htr); work the section in brackets ( ) twice; 1ch, miss next htr, work 2htr, 1ch and 2htr all into 2nd htr of next corner group, repeat from * twice more, (1ch, miss next htr, 1htr into next htr) twice, 1ch, join last ch worked to 2nd of first 2ch. You should have three 1ch spaces between each corner group.
4th round Using white, slip stitch over first 2htr and into the 1ch space at corner, 2ch, work 1htr, 1ch and 2htr all into same space, *1htr into each of next 2htr, (1htr into next 1ch space, 1htr into next htr) 3 times, 1htr into next htr, 2htr, 1ch and 2htr all into 1ch space at corner, repeat from * to the end of the round, but do not work the last corner group at the end of the last repeat, join the last htr worked to the 2nd of the first 2ch with a slip stitch.
Fasten off.
You should have worked 9htr between each corner group.
5th round Join blue to 1ch space at one corner, 2ch, now work 1htr, 1ch and 2htr all into same space, *(1ch, miss next htr, 1htr into next htr) to within 2nd htr of next corner group, 1ch, miss next htr, now work 2htr, 1ch and 2htr all into 1ch space at corner, repeat from * all round, but do not work the last corner group at the end of the last repeat; join the last ch worked to the 2nd of the first 2ch with a slip stitch. There should be 7 spaces between each corner group.
6th round Using blue, slip stitch over first 2htr and into the 1ch space at corner, 2ch, work 1htr, 1ch and 2htr all into same space, *1htr into each of next 2htr, (1htr into next 1ch space, 1htr into next htr) to within 2nd htr of next corner group, 1htr into next htr, 2htr, 1ch and 2htr all into 1ch space at corner, repeat from * to the end of the round, but do not work the last corner group at the end of the last repeat, join the last htr worked to the 2nd of the first 2ch with a slip stitch. Fasten off. There should be 17htr on each side between corner groups.
Continue to work the 5th and 6th rounds alternately working in a colour sequence of 2 rounds yellow, 2 rounds green, 2

rounds red, 2 rounds white and 2 rounds blue until the 2nd round of the 3rd white stripe has been worked. Fasten off. This completes one square.
Work 3 more squares in the same way.

To make the plain square
Using blue throughout, work the first circle and first and 2nd rounds as given for striped square.
3rd round Slip stitch into top of 2nd htr of 3htr at corner, work 2ch which will count as first htr, now work 1 htr, 1ch and 2htr all into same htr for corner group, *(1ch, miss next htr, 1 htr into next htr) twice, 1ch, miss next htr, work 2htr, 1ch and 2htr all into 2nd htr of next corner group, repeat from * twice more, (1ch, miss next htr, 1htr into next htr) twice, 1ch, join last ch to 2nd of first 2ch worked.
There will be three 1ch spaces between each corner group.
4th round Slip stitch over first 2htr and into the 1ch space at corner, 2ch, work 1htr, 1ch and 2htr all into same space, *1htr into each of next 2htr, (1htr into next 1ch space, 1htr into next htr) 3 times, 1htr into next htr, 2htr, 1ch and 2htr all into 1ch space at corner, repeat from * to the end of the round, but do not work the last corner group at the end of the last repeat, join the last htr worked to the 2nd of the first 2ch with a slip stitch.
5th round Slip stitch over first 2htr and into the 1ch space at corner, 2ch, now work 1htr, 1ch and 2htr all into same space, *(1ch, miss next htr, 1htr into next htr) to within 2nd htr of next corner group, 1ch, miss next htr, now work 2htr, 1ch and 2htr all into 1ch space at corner, repeat from * all round, but do not work the last corner group at the end of the last repeat, join the last ch worked to the 2nd of the first 2ch with a slip stitch.
Continue working rounds 4 and 5 until square measures the same as the striped square. Fasten off.
This completes the first square.
Work three more squares in the same way.

To make up cushion
Darn all loose ends to the wrong side of each square, keeping each colour in its own stripe.
With the right side of two striped squares facing, using white yarn and a flat seam, join one edge of the squares together. Join the other two striped squares in the same way. Now join these two pieces together to make one large square. Join the plain squares in the same way.

The edging
With right side facing, insert hook into one corner space and draw a loop of blue through, 2ch, work 1htr, 1ch and 2htr all into same space, *(1ch, miss next htr, 1htr into next htr) along edge to corner, 1ch, miss next htr, work 2htr, 1ch and

2htr all into corner space, repeat from *
all round, but do not work corner group
at end of last repeat, join last 1ch worked
to 2nd of the first 2ch with a slip stitch.
Next round Work as given for 4th round
of plain square. Fasten off.
Work round outer edge of other square in
the same way.
Darn in all loose ends on wrong side of
work.

To join the squares together

With wrong sides facing join on blue ;
working through double thickness work a
row of dc round 3 sides of cover, working
1dc into each htr and 2dc into each
space at corner. Fasten off. Insert
cushion pad, then join the remaining
seam in the same way.
You could insert a zip fastener into this
side if required.

Diagonally striped cushion

Size
Our cover has been made to fit a cushion
pad 91.5cm by 91.5cm square.
The cover measures approximately
89cm by 89cm square – 2.5cm less than
pad. Each square measures approximately
42cm by 42cm square, excluding edging.

Materials
28 x 50g balls of Sunbeam Aran
   Tweed in dark brown, A
   11 balls in each of beige, B and grey, C
   4.00mm crochet hook
   A cushion pad 91.5cm by 91.5cm
   square

Tension
18htr and 11 rows to 10cm worked on a
4.00mm hook.

Note If you wish to alter the size of the
cover to fit a different-sized pad or to fit
an existing cushion, measure the width of
your cushion pad and make your cover
2.5cm less. For example a cushion
measuring 63.5cm by 63.5cm square will
need a cover measuring 61cm by 61cm
square. Allow 2.5cm all round for edging
and subtract this figure from the total
size so that the area for remaining squares
will be 56cm x 56cm. Each square will
therefore measure approximately 28cm x
28cm.

To make the striped square
Each square is worked in stripes on one
half, with the other half being worked
in one colour only. Take care when
changing colours to avoid making a hole
between the stitches.
Using 4.00mm hook and B, make 10ch,
join with a slip stitch to first ch to form
a circle.
1st round Work 2ch, which will count
as first htr, then work 15htr into the

circle ; join the last htr to the 2nd of the
first 2ch worked with a slip stitch.
There are 16htr.
2nd round Work 2ch, which will count
as first htr, then work 2 htr into the same
place as slip stitch – 1 corner formed,
*work 1 htr into each of the next 3 htr,
3 htr all into next htr – corner formed,
repeat from asterisk (*) twice more,
work 1 htr into each of next 3 htr, join
the last htr worked to top of the first
2ch to complete the round. Commence
striped pattern.
3rd round Using B, work 1 slip stitch
into 2nd htr of group at corner, 2 ch,
1 htr into same place as slip stitch, (1 ch,
miss next htr, 1 htr into next htr) work
the section in brackets ( ) twice ; 1 ch
miss next htr, now work 2htr, 1ch and
2htr all into 2nd htr of next corner group,
(1ch, miss next htr, 1htr into next htr)
twice, 1ch, miss next htr, work 2htr into
2nd htr of the next corner group, join
in second colour by drawing C through
working loop. Cut off B. Complete the
round in C by working 2htr into same
htr as last 2htr, (1ch, miss next htr, 1htr,
into next htr) twice, 1ch, miss next htr,
now work 2htr, 1ch and 2htr all into
2nd htr of the next corner group,
(1ch, miss next htr, work 1htr into next
htr) twice, 1ch, miss next htr work 2htr
into same htr as first 2htr, 1ch, insert
hook into the 2nd of the first 2ch, and
draw B through. Cut off C.
There should be three 1ch spaces
between each corner group.
4th round Using B, work 2ch, 1htr into
1ch space at corner, 1htr into each of
next 2htr, (1htr into next 1ch space, 1htr
into next htr) 3 times, 1htr into next htr,
now work 2htr, 1ch and 2htr all into
corner space, 1htr into each of next 2htr,
(1htr into next 1ch space, 1htr into next
htr) 3 times, 1htr into next htr, 2htr into
1ch space at corner. Join in second
colour by drawing C through working
loop. Cut off B. Complete round in C by
working 2htr into same place as last
2htr, 1htr into each of next 2htr, (1htr
into next space, 1htr into next htr) 3
times, 1htr into next htr, now work 2htr,
1ch and 2htr all into next space at
corner, 1htr into each of next 2htr, (1htr
into next 1ch space, 1htr into next htr) 3
times, 1htr into next htr, 2htr into same
space as first 2htr, 1ch, insert hook into
the 2nd of the first 2ch and draw B
through. Cut off C.
5th round Work 2ch, 1htr into 1ch space
at corner, (1ch, miss next htr, 1htr into
next htr) to within 2nd htr of corner
group, 1ch, miss next htr, now work
2htr, 1ch and 2htr all into 1ch space at
corner, (1ch, miss next htr, 1htr into
next htr) to within 2nd htr of next corner
group, 1ch, 2htr into 1ch space at
corner. Join in 2nd colour by drawing A
through working loop. Cut off B.
Complete round in A, finishing by

working 2htr into same space as first
2htr, 1ch, insert hook into the 2nd of the
first 2ch and draw B through. Cut off A.
6th round Work 2ch, 1htr into 1ch space
at corner, continue to work as for 4th
round, working 1htr into each htr and
1ch space and 2htr, 1ch and 2htr all into
1ch space at corners. Remember to
change from B to A at corner, as before.
Continue to work stripes of 2 rounds in
each colour, keeping one half in B and
working the other half in colour sequence
of C, A and B throughout.
Make sure that the pattern is correct when
changing colours at corners. As the
square increases in size the length of each
stripe will also be extended. Continue to
work the square until it measures
approximately 42cm square. Fasten off.
Make one more square in the same way.
Make two squares, keeping the stripe
sequence the same but working the
plain half in C instead of B.
These 4 squares form the top of the
cushion.

To make the plain squares
Using A only throughout, work 4
squares as given for plain square on
multi-striped cover.

To make up
Darn all loose ends to the wrong side
of each square.
With the right side of two striped
squares facing, using the corresponding
colour and a flat seam join one edge of
the squares. Join the other two striped
squares in the same way.
Now join these 2 pieces together,
matching the stripes, to make one
larger square.
Join the plain squares in the same way.

The edging
With right side facing insert hook into
one corner space and draw a loop of A
through, 2ch, work 1htr, 1ch and 2htr all
into same space, *(1ch, miss next htr,
1htr into next htr) along edge to corner,
1ch, miss next htr, work 2htr, 1ch and
2htr all into corner space, repeat from *
all round but do not work corner group at
end of last repeat, join last 1ch worked to
2nd of the first 2ch with a slip stitch.
Next round Work as given for 4th round
of plain square. Fasten off. Work round
outer edge of other square in the same
way. Darn in loose ends on wrong side.

To join the squares together
With wrong sides facing join on A and,
working through double thickness, work
a row of dc round 3 sides of cover,
working 1dc into each htr and 2dc into
each space at corner. Fasten off. Insert
cushion pad, then join the remaining
seam in the same way.
You could insert a zip fastener into this
side if required.

Step-by-step course – 15

Joining lace motifs with crochet

Once you have completed the first motif of a lacy fabric, you can join the second and all subsequent motifs while working the last round of each. Working in this way not only maintains the continuity of the lace pattern but also greatly enhances the motifs themselves.

The beautiful bedspreads and lace table-cloths characteristic of traditional crochet are frequently worked in this way. Crochet patterns usually give detailed instructions on how to join the particular motifs you are working. They may appear complicated, but don't be put off.

If you follow the instructions carefully you will get beautiful results. The step-by-step instructions given here are for joining two of the motifs used in the tablecloth featured in this course, but the principle is the same for any motif with lace edges.

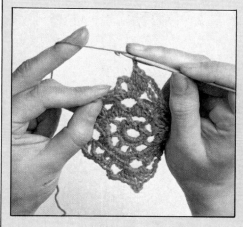

1 Begin the sample by working the first motif from the table cloth instructions and the first 5 rounds of the second motif.

2 Hold the first motif behind the 2nd motif with the wrong side of each square facing. Match 1 corner picot of the first motif to the working loop at the end of the 5th round on the 2nd motif.

3 Work 1 double crochet through the corner picot of the first motif to join the squares together. The double crochet will count as the corner picot of the 2nd motif.

4 Leave the first motif. Make 2 chains and then work 3 treble into each of the next 3 treble on the 2nd motif, thus continuing to work the 6th round of the 2nd motif.

5 Hold the 2 motifs together again, matching the block of 3 treble just worked with the corresponding 3 treble on the first motif. Work 1 slip stitch into the first chain of the next 5 chain loop on to the first motif.

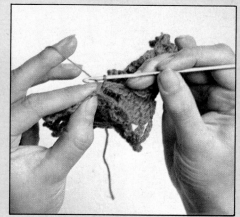

6 Leave the first motif. Work 4 chain and then 1 slip stitch into the next double crochet on the second motif.

continued

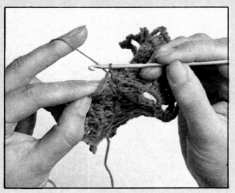

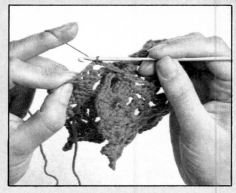

7 Work 1 chain, hold the 2 motifs together as before and work 1 double crochet into the next 4 chain picot on the first motif.

8 Leave the first motif and work 1 chain. Miss the next double crochet on the 2nd motif and then work 1 slip stitch into the next double crochet of the same motif.

9 Work 4 chain. Hold the 2 motifs together and then work 1 slip stitch into the last chain before the next 3 treble block on the first motif.

10 Leave the first motif. Work 1 treble into each of the next 3 treble on the 2nd motif. Work 2 chain. Hold the 2 motifs together and work 1 double crochet into the centre of the picot on the next corner of the first motif. One side of each square has now been joined.

11 Complete the 6th round of the 2nd motif in the same way as given for the second motif of the tablecloth. Join the last stitch to the first with a slip stitch.

12 Where the motifs are being joined in strips, each consecutive motif should be joined in the same way. Remember to work the first 5 rounds of the 2nd motif each time.

Joining lace motifs to make a square fabric

Where two sides of a motif are to be joined to produce a square fabric, the working method is exactly the same as for joining them in a strip, but it is important to work the joins in the correct order, so that the motifs are crocheted together evenly. The step-by-step instructions that follow relate to the table-cloth pattern, but apply to other square fabrics as well.

1 After completing the first row, or strip, of motifs, work the first five rounds of the first motif of the second row. Join one side of this motif to the lower edge of the first motif of the first row. Complete the sixth round.

2 Work the first five rounds of the next motif. With the wrong side of both motifs facing, hold the first and second motifs of this row together so that the bottom left-hand corner of the first motif corresponds to the working loop on the second motif.

3 Work 1 double crochet into the first corner picot of the first motif. This double crochet will count as the first corner picot of the 6th round on the second motif.

4 Now join the two motifs together on this side in the same way as before, making sure that you work the last double crochet on this side into the centre of the corner where the first 3 motifs meet. You will be working the 6th round of the 2nd motif at the same time as joining the two motifs together.

5 Turn the work so that the first row of motifs is at the top of your work and the first motif of the 2nd row on the right-hand side.

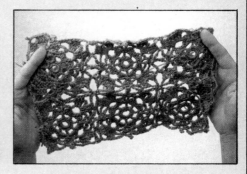

6 Now join the top of the 2nd motif of the 2nd row to the bottom of the 2nd motif of the first row in the same way as before, beginning by working 2 chain and then 3 treble into the first 3 treble on the 2nd motif.

7 Complete the 6th round of the 2nd motif, working round the remaining 2 sides of the square and joining the last stitch to the corner picot on the first motif.

8 Work subsequent joins in the same way, making sure that you always work from the bottom left-hand corner of the motif to the right of the one to be joined, then up and across to the top left-hand corner of the motif being joined. In this way each motif will be joined correctly to the one before.

Joining simple squares with lace crochet

Square motifs with straight sides can also be joined with crochet by working a picot or decorative edging round the first square and then using the same edging to join the following motifs together. Once you have mastered the basic technique you will be able to join any square in the same way, using a variety of picot edgings. This will enable you to combine a motif and edging of your choice and create your own fabric.

The edging you use will depend on the size of motif you wish to make and the type of yarn being used. To follow these step-by-step instructions, first make two granny squares (Crochet Course 14 page 199). Work only 3 rounds for each motif.

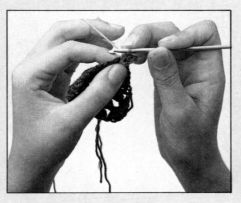

1 With the right side of one motif facing, join the yarn to any corner space and make 4 chain. Work 1 double crochet into the 3rd chain from the hook to form a picot point. Now work 1 double crochet into the same corner space. This step will now be referred to as a 4 chain corner picot.

2 Work 1 double crochet into the next treble, then 4 chain and then 1 double crochet into the following treble. This makes one 4 chain loop.

continued

3 Work 4 chain and then 1 double crochet into the next chain loop on the previous round, making the 2nd 4 chain loop on the side of the square.

4 Repeat steps 2 and 3 once more and then step 2 once again. There will now be 5 loops on this side of the square.

5 Work 1 double crochet into the chain loop of the previous round at the next corner. Now work a 4 chain corner picot into the same loop.

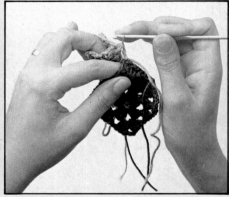

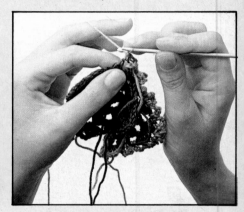

6 Continue to work all round the square in the same way, making 5 loops on each side and one 4 chain corner loop on each corner. Join the last double crochet to the first chain worked at the beginning of the round. This completes the decorative edging for the first motif.

7 With the right side of the 2nd motif facing, join the yarn to any corner space and work 2 chain. Hold the first and 2nd motifs together with the wrong sides of each facing, and work a slip stitch into the top of the picot point at one corner on the first motif.

8 Work 2 chain and then 1 double crochet into the same space on the 2nd motif to complete the corner on the 2nd motif.

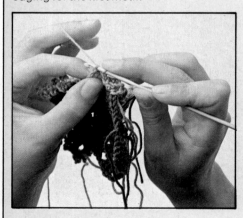

9 Work 1 double crochet into the next stitch on the 2nd motif, then 2 chain. Hold the motifs together and work a slip stitch into the top of the first loop on the first motif, working through the stitch rather than under the loop.

10 Work 2 chain and then 1 double crochet into the next treble on the 2nd motif. Now work 2 chain, then 1 slip stitch into the top of the next loop on the first motif.

11 Work 2 chain and then 1 double crochet into the next chain loop on the 2nd motif.

Paul Williams

Paul Williams

12 Repeat steps 9 to 11 once more. Now work 1 double crochet into the next stitch.

13 Work 2 chain and then 1 slip stitch into the last loop on the side of the first motif. Now work 2 chain and 1 double crochet into the next stitch on the 2nd motif. Work one more double crochet into the next corner space on the 2nd motif and join it to the picot on the first motif as before, thus joining the two sides together.

14 Complete the picot edging round the remaining 3 sides of the 2nd square in the same way as given for the first motif. When joining the motifs on 2 sides, remember to start at the bottom left-hand corner of the motif to the right of the one being joined, then up and across to the top left-hand corner of the motif being joined.

The lacy look

Small motifs worked in a fine thread and crocheted together in strips make a lovely table cover. Lay it over a plain cloth in a contrasting colour to show off its delicate lines and texture.

Size
77cm at the widest part.

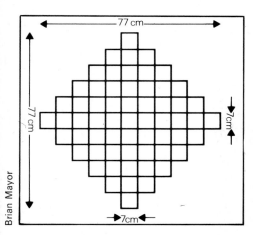

Brian Mayor

Materials
Total of 150g of crochet cotton such as Twilleys Lyscordet
2.00mm crochet hook

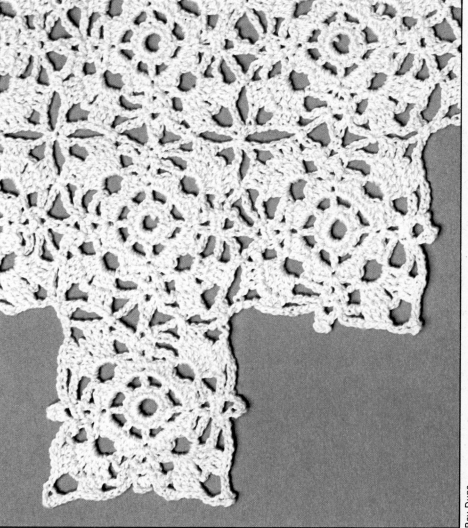

Ray Duns

Tension

1 motif measures 7cm square on 2.00mm hook.

First motif

Make 6ch, join with a ss to first ch to form circle.

1st round 2ch to count as first dc, work 15dc into circle, join with a ss to second of first 2ch.

2nd round 4ch to count as first htr and 2ch, *miss next dc, 1htr into next dc, 2ch, rep from * 6 times more, join with a ss to second of first 4ch.

3rd round Work *1dc, 1htr, 1tr, 1htr and 1dc all into next ch sp, 1ch, rep from * to end, join with a ss to first dc. 8 petals.

4th round 2ch to count as first htr, *3ch, 1dc into tr of next petal, 4ch, 1dc into tr of next petal, 3ch, 1htr into 1ch sp before next petal, 2ch, 1htr into same ch sp, rep from * twice more, 3ch, 1dc into tr of next petal, 4ch, 1dc into tr of next petal, 3ch, 1htr into last 1ch sp after last petal, 2ch, join with a ss to second of first 2ch.

5th round 1ch, *4ch, now work 3tr, 3ch and 3tr all into next 4ch sp to form corner, 4ch, 1dc into next htr, 1dc into next 2ch sp, 1dc into next htr, rep from * twice more, 4ch, now work 3tr, 3ch and 3tr all into next 4ch sp, 4ch, 1dc into next htr, 1dc into next 2ch sp, join with a ss to first ch.

6th round 1ch, *5ch, 1tr into each of next 3tr, 5ch, insert hook into 3rd ch from hook to form a little loop and work 1dc to form picot – called 5ch picot – 2ch, 1tr into each of next 3tr, 5ch, ss into next dc, 4ch, insert hook into 3rd ch from hook and work 1dc to form picot – called 4ch picot – 1ch, miss next dc, ss into next dc ; rep from * twice more, 5ch, 1tr into each of next 3tr, work a 5ch picot, 2ch, 1tr into each of next 3tr, 5ch, ss into next dc, work a 4ch picot, 1ch, join with a ss to first ch. Fasten off.

Second motif

Work as given for first motif to end of round 5.

6th round (joining round) 1ch, *5ch, 1tr into each of next 3tr, 2ch, with right side of completed motif facing right side of second motif, which is to be joined, work 1dc into 5ch picot at corner of first motif, 2ch, 1tr into each of next 3tr of second motif, ss into first of 5ch after last tr on first motif, 4ch, ss into next dc of second motif, 1ch, 1dc into 4ch picot of first motif, 1ch, miss next dc on second motif, ss into next dc on second motif, 4ch, ss into last ch before next 3tr on first motif, 1tr into each of next 3tr on second motif, 2ch, 1dc into 5ch picot at corner of first motif, 2ch. One side has been joined. Complete motif as given for first motif. Fasten off.

☐ Make a strip of 11 joined motifs.
☐ Make and join 50 more motifs, placing them as shown in diagram. When two sides have to be joined, join the first side to the corresponding motif on the preceding strip and the second side to the preceding motif of the same strip.
☐ Pin out and press with a warm iron over a damp cloth.

Step-by-step course – 16

*Working flat, circular motifs
*An openwork motif
*Working continuous rounds
*Making a simple tassel
*Patterns for three hats

Working flat, circular motifs

Working circles in crochet is an important technique, since it is widely used to produce a variety of household items and fabrics.

The basic circle is made of a small number of stitches that are then increased evenly on each round until the motif is the size required. You can use any of a variety of yarns – dishcloth cotton, raffia and string, as well as fine crochet cotton – to achieve a variety of different effects with the same basic shape. In this course we show you how to work two of the simplest round motifs. Once you have mastered the basic technique, you can progress to a more complicated design.

1 Use a double knitting yarn and 4.50mm hook for this sample. Make 5 chain and join them into a circle with a slipstitch.

2 Make 3 chain to count as the first treble of the round. Now work 15 treble into the centre of the circle. You may have to push the stitches together while working to fit them all into the circle.

3 Join the last treble to the 3rd of the first 3 chain with a slip stitch. There will now be 16 treble in the circle, counting the first 3 chain as 1 treble.

4 Make 3 chain. Now work 2 treble into each stitch all the way round the circle. Complete the round by working 1 treble into the stitch at the base of the first 3 chain, and join this to the top of these chain as before. There should now be 32 treble worked in the 2nd round.

5 Begin the 3rd round by working three chain as before. Now work 1 treble into the next treble and then 2 treble into the next stitch on the previous round. The first increase has now been made.

6 Work round circle in the same way, working 2 treble into every other stitch. Work last treble into stitch at base of chain. Join last stitch to first 3 chain as before. There should be 48 treble in the circle.

7 Work the next round in the same way, but work 2 treble into every 3rd stitch, instead of every alternate stitch as on the previous round.

8 Work the last treble into the stitch at the base of the first 3 chain. Join with a slip stitch as before. There should now be 64 stitches in the circle.

continued

Paul Williams

Note Patterns for flat motifs are carefully devised to ensure that the motif does lie flat. If you are adapting or designing a motif of your own, you will need to pay special attention to the number of increases you make on each round : with too few increased stitches, the motif will curl up at the edges and with too many increased stitches, the finished motif will have a fluted appearance.

9 Continue to increase 16 stitches on each round in the same way, working 1 more treble between each increase on every subsequent round.

10 Work a total of 6 rounds for a motif approximately 16cm in diameter. There should be a total of 96 treble worked in the last round.

An openwork motif

This openwork motif demonstrates the use of spaces to make a flat circular shape, using the spaces for increasing on each round. Try working the motif in a different kind of material, such as a thick cotton or string ; or work each round in a different colour to vary the completed motif.

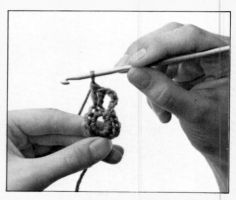

1 Make 6 chain and join them into a ring with a slip stitch. Make 1 chain and then work 12 double crochet into the centre of the ring. You may have to push the stitches together while working in order to fit them into the circle.

2 Make 5 chain to count as the first treble and 2 chain space of the 2nd round. Miss the next stitch of the previous round and work 2 treble into the next stitch.

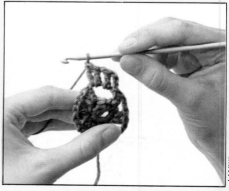

3 Work 2 chain. Miss the next stitch and work 2 treble into the following stitch. Repeat this step 3 times more.

4 Now work 2 chain and then 1 treble into the stitch at the base of the first 5 chain to complete the round. Join the last stitch to the 3rd of the first 5 chain with a slip stitch. There should be 6 groups of treble in all.

5 Begin the 3rd round with 3 chain. Now work 1 treble followed by 1 chain and then 2 treble all into the first space in the previous round.

Paul Williams

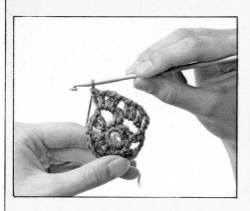

6 Make 1 chain ; then work 2 treble followed by 1 chain and 2 treble, all into the next chain space in the previous round.

7 Repeat step 6 into each space all the way round the circle. Complete the round with 1 chain and join this with a slip stitch to the top of the first 3 chain. There are now 12 groups of treble with 1 chain between each. This completes the 3rd round.

8 To begin the 4th round in the correct place, work a slip stitch across the next stitch and into the first chain space so that you will work the first stitch from this space.

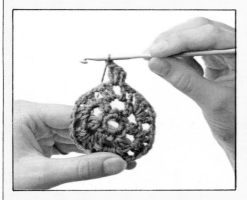

9 Work 3 chain for the first stitch and then 2 treble into the same space as the first 3 chain, making a group of 3 treble. Now work 1 chain.

10 Continue to work round the circle in the same way, working 3 treble into each space with 1 chain between each group of treble.

11 Work the last group of this round into the space before the block of 2 treble below the first 3 chain. Join the last chain to top of the first 3 chain with a slip stitch.

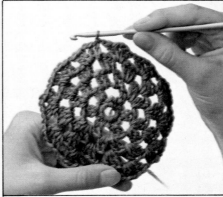

12 Begin the 5th round by working a slip stitch across the first treble block of the row below and into the first chain space. Now work 3 chain.

13 Repeat the 3rd round all round the circle, so that there are twenty-four 2-treble blocks. Join the last chain to the top of the first 3 chain with a slip stitch.

14 To make the motif bigger, repeat the 3rd and 4th rounds alternately until the motif is the required size. To work each round in a different colour, break off 1 colour at the end of the round and join next colour to first chain space of next round, so you need not work slip stitches at the beginning of the rounds.

Paul Williams

Working continuous rounds

An alternative way to work a circle is to crochet continuously round the centre circle, leaving the ends of each round unjoined, thus creating a spiral effect on your fabric. By working in this way it is possible to produce a six-sided motif in either a solid fabric – using double crochet or half treble – or a more open fabric with a lace pattern incorporated into the design. Try making several motifs, each in a different colour, and sewing them together to make an attractive piece of patchwork. This method of working is frequently used as a form of decorative shaping on the crown of a hat or beret, where the lines formed by the increases create a 'star' effect on the very top of the crown.

Our sample has been worked in a double knitting yarn with a 4.50mm hook.

1 Make 6 chain and join them into a circle with a slip stitch. Work 1 chain. Now work 12 double crochet into the centre of the circle. Do not join this or any of the following rounds.

2 Now work 2 double crochet into each double crochet of the previous round so that there are 24 stitches in all. Check at this point that you have the correct number of stitches.

3 Now work 1 double crochet into each of the next 3 double crochet of the previous round, and then work 3 chain.

4 Miss the next double crochet and work 1 double crochet into each of the next 3 double crochet. At this point, you have made the first space on the round. Now work 3 chain.

5 Continue to work all the way round the circle in the same way, working 3 double crochet between each space and missing 1 double crochet below each 3 chain worked until there are 5 chain spaces in all. Complete round by working 3 chain after last 3 double crochet. These chain will count as the 6th space on this round.

6 Begin the 4th round by missing the first double crochet and then working 1 double crochet into each of the next 3 stitches. Now work 2 double crochet into the first 3 chain space on the previous round.

7 Work 3 chain and then 1 double crochet into each of the next 3 stitches, followed by 2 double crochet into the next space. The first space of the 4th round is thus worked to the left of the space in the previous round to begin the spiral shape.

8 Complete this round, working in the same way all round the circle, ending with 3 chain, so that you have worked 5 complete spaces with the last 3 chain counting as the 6th space as before.

9 Work the 5th round by missing the first double crochet and working 1 double crochet into each of the next 4 stitches. Now work 2 double crochet into the next space.

10 Work 4 chain and then repeat step 9 once more. Continue to work round the circle in the same way with four double crochet between each space, and end the round with 4 chain so that you will have worked 5 complete spaces with the last 4 chain counting as the 6th space as on the previous round.

11 Begin the 6th round by missing the first double crochet of the next block and working 1 double crochet into each of the next 5 double crochet. Now work 2 double crochet into the next chain space, followed by 4 chain.

12 Repeat step 11 all the way round the circle until you have worked 5 spaces with the last 4 chain counting as the 6th space as before.

13 Work the 7th round by missing the first double crochet and then working 1 double crochet into each of the next remaining double crochet in the next block, followed by 2 double crochet into the next space and then 5 chain. Work in the same way all round the circle, making 5 spaces as before and counting the last 5 chain as the 6th space.

14 Continue to repeat the last round 5 times more to make a motif approx. 20cm in diameter, a!ways missing the first stitch on each block of double crochet in the previous round and then working into each remaining stitch in the block. There will be one more stitch worked in each block on every round.

Making a simple tassel

Follow these step-by-step instructions to make the tassel for the blue hat featured on page 72. You can alter the size of the tassel by changing the length of yarn cut and the number of lengths you use.

1 Cut 16 lengths of yarn, each approximately 12cm long. Fold the yarn in half.

2 Cut a length of yarn at least 30cm long and tie one end firmly round the centre of the lengths of yarn.

continued

Paul Williams

continued: Making a simple tassel

3 Wind the remaining length of yarn several times round the top of the tassel just below the centre fold, leaving enough yarn to be threaded into a needle.

4 Thread the yarn into a blunt-ended needle and insert the needle under the yarn wound round the tassel, and up through the middle of the tassel.

5 Catch the yarn with a slip stitch in the middle of the head of the tassel and then take it down through the centre so that it becomes one of the ends. Trim the ends if necessary.

Hats on !

If you've got a head for hats, make up one – or all three – of these crocheted charmers. Worked in rounds, they can be varied in all sorts of ways to team up with just about anything in your wardrobe.

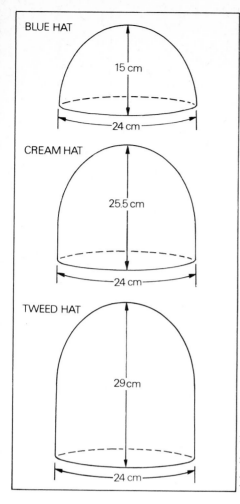

BLUE HAT

15 cm

24 cm

CREAM HAT

25.5 cm

24 cm

TWEED HAT

29 cm

24 cm

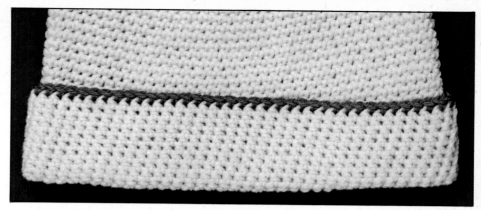

John Hutchinson

Sizes
To fit average size head : other measurements are shown on the diagrams.

Materials
Blue hat : total of 75g of double knitting yarn such as Patons Superwash Wool double knitting
Cream hat : total of 125g of double knitting yarn such as Patons Superwash Wool double knitting
An oddment of blue yarn
Tweed hat : total of 100g of double knitting yarn such as Patons Bracken Tweed
3.50mm and 4.00mm crochet hooks

Tension
18dc and 20 rows to 10cm.

Blue hat
*Using 4.00rnm hook make 3ch, join with a ss to first ch to form a circle.
Next round Work 6dc into circle ; mark the first of these 6dc to denote the beginning of the round.
Working in continuous rounds, proceed as follows :
☐ Work 2dc into each of next 6dc to increase 6dc.
☐ Work (1dc into next dc, 2dc into next

dc) 6 times.
☐ Work (1dc into each of next 2dc, 2dc into next dc) 6 times.
☐ Work (1dc into each of next 3dc, 2dc into next dc) 6 times.
☐ Work (1dc into each of next 4dc, 2dc into next dc) 6 times.
☐ Continue to increase in this way until 11dc have been worked between each increase ; you should have 76dc. *
☐ Work straight on these 76dc until work measures 15cm measured at centre.
☐ Change to 3.50mm hook and work 1 round. Fasten off.

Cord
☐ Using 3.50mm hook make 60ch, ss into each ch to end. Fasten off.
☐ Make 2 tassels and sew one to each end of cord.
☐ Sew centre of cord to top of hat.

Cream hat
☐ Using cream, work as given for blue hat from * to *.
☐ Work straight on these 76dc until work measures 25.5cm measured at centre. Fasten off.
☐ With wrong side of work facing join on blue and work 1 round of dc. Fasten off.
☐ Turn back 6cm for brim.

Ray Duns

Tweed hat
☐ Work as given for blue hat from * to *
☐ Work straight on these 76dc until work measures 29cm measured at centre. Fasten off.
☐ Fold back 15cm for brim.

Step-by-step course – 17

More about motifs

Now that you have mastered the basic principles of working a square motif, try making this pretty square with the Catherine wheel centre. The centre of the motif is worked in a circular shape with the corners and straight sides only being worked on the last two rounds – unlike the granny square, in which the four corners of the motif are made on the first round.

Our motif has been worked in a 4-ply yarn using a 3.50mm hook. Try making the same motif in several colours or using different yarns and hook sizes to see the variety of effects you can achieve. The same motif worked in a fine cotton will be very different when worked in a chunky yarn with a large hook.

1 Make 8 chain and join into a circle with a slip stitch. Now work 2 chain to count as the first treble, followed by 15 treble into the circle. Join the last treble to the first 2 chain with a slip stitch. Join each round in the same way.

2 Make 5 chain to count as the first treble and 2 chain space of the next round. Now work 1 treble followed by 2 chain into each stitch all round the circle. Join the last chain to the top of the 3 chain at the beginning of the round.

3 Work 3 chain to count as the first treble of the next round. Now work 2 treble into the first 2 chain space. This will be the first block of treble.

4 Work 1 chain, then 3 treble into the next 2 chain space.

5 Repeat step 4 all the way round the circle so that there are 16 blocks of trebles with 1 chain between each block. Join last chain to top of the first 3 chain.

6 Work 3 chain and then 1 double crochet into the next 1 chain space. Repeat this action twice more so that there are 3 loops on this side of the circle.

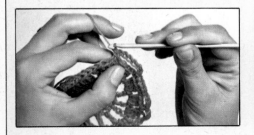

7 Work the first corner of the square by making 6 chain and then working 1 double crochet into the next 1 chain space.

8 Repeat steps 6 and 7 all round the motif so that there are three 3-chain loops on each side with a 6-chain loop at each corner, and 1 double crochet worked into each 1 chain space. Join the last chain to the base of the first three chain.

9 Work 3 chain to count as the first treble of the next round and then 2 treble into the first 2 chain space.

10 Now work 3 treble into each of the next two 3-chain loops on the side of the square.

11 Work 5 treble followed by 2 chain and 5 treble all into the next 6-chain loop at the corner.

12 Continue to work round the square in the same way, with three blocks of three treble on each side and 5 treble, 2 chain and 5 treble all into the 6-chain loop at each of the remaining 3 corners. Join the last treble to the top of the first 3 treble. This completes the motif.

Working a picot edging

There are various picot edgings which can be worked with a crochet hook directly on to the edge of the fabric, the simplest being that featured on the baby's carrying cape in this course. As they are worked into the edge of the fabric, they can be used not only as a decorative trimming but also as a means of neatening an uneven edge or hem on a crocheted or knitted fabric. They can be worked in either rows or rounds in any thickness of yarn, from a fine cotton for a delicate trimming on table linens to a thick wool for a chunky cardigan or tabard.

Our sample has been worked in a 4-ply yarn on a piece of double crochet fabric. Once you have mastered the working technique, try using a fine hook and crochet cotton for a different effect.

1 With the right side of the work facing, make 5 chain at the right-hand edge of the fabric to count as the first half treble and 2 chain space.

2 Miss the next 2 stitches and then work 1 half treble into the next stitch.

3 Make 2 chain and then repeat step 2 once more.

4 Repeat step 3 all along the edge of the fabric, working the last half treble into the turning chain at the end of the last row of the main fabric. You have now worked a series of 2 chain spaces with 1 half treble between each space.

5 Turn. Work 1 double crochet into the first space, inserting the hook from front to back under the 2 chain worked in the previous row.

continued

Fred Mancini

6 Make 3 chain and then work 1 slip stitch into the first of these 3 chain to form the picot point.

7 Work another double crochet into the same space, as before, so that 1 picot block has now been completed.

8 Continue to work 1 picot block in exactly the same way into each chain space to the end of the row to complete the edging.

Joining motifs with a slip stitch

Square motifs with straight side edges can be joined together with a slip stitch to make a very firm seam with a raised appearance. Use this method of seaming on something like a chunky rug or blanket to make sure that the motifs are joined firmly together and to make a feature of the seams.

1 Hold the two motifs to be joined with the wrong sides together and insert the hook through both corners.

2 Draw a loop of yarn through both corners and make 1 chain to hold the yarn in place.

3 Work 1 slip stitch into the next stitch, working through both thicknesses.

4 Continue to work 1 slip stitch into each stitch along the edge of the motifs, taking care to work into the corresponding stitch on each motif.

5 When laid flat the seams thus joined are raised, producing a kind of lattice effect.

Cosy hooded cape

Sizes
To fit a baby up to 3 months old.
Length to shoulder, 49cm.
Length of hood to shoulder, 21cm.

Materials
*Total of 300g of double knitting yarn
in a random shade such as Peter
Pan Darling DK Random*
3.00mm crochet hook
3.50mm crochet hook
1 button

What could be easier to make – or more comfortable for baby to wear – than this pretty cape? The pastel random yarn gives a soft effect to the motifs, which are sewn together in a simple rectangular shape. The picot edging is worked after the hood and cape have been joined.

Serge Krouglikoff/accessories from Fenwicks

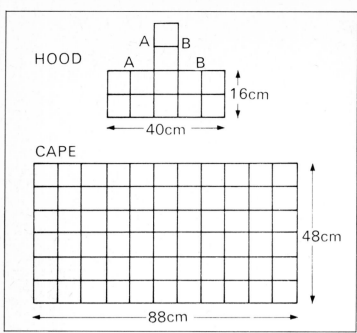

HOOD

A   B

A   B

16cm

40cm

CAPE

48cm

88cm

Tension

1 motif measures 8cm square worked on a 3.50mm hook.

The motif

Using 3.50mm hook, make 6ch, join with a ss to first ch to form a circle.

1st round Work 3ch to count as first tr, then work 19tr into the circle, join the last tr to the 3rd of the first 3ch with a ss.

2nd round 1ch to count as first dc, 1htr into next tr, work 1tr, 3ch and 1tr all into next tr – corner formed, 1htr into next tr, *1dc into each of next 2tr, 1htr into next tr, now work 1tr, 3ch and 2tr all into next tr – corner formed, 1htr into next tr, rep from * twice more, 1dc into next tr, join last dc to the first ch with a ss.

3rd round 3ch, 1tr into each of next 2sts, work 2tr, 3ch and 2tr all into loop at corner – called 1 gr, *1tr into each of next 6sts, work 1 gr into centre of loop at corner, rep from * twice more, 1 tr into each of last 3sts, join last tr to 3rd of first 3ch with a ss.

4th round 3ch, 1tr into each of next 4tr, 1gr into centre of gr at corner, *1tr into each of next 10tr, work 1gr into centre of gr at corner, rep from * twice more, 1tr into each of next 5tr, join last tr to 3rd of first 3ch with a ss. Fasten off.

☐ Make 65 more motifs in same way for cape and then make 12 for hood.

Cape

Darn in all loose ends to wrong side of motifs. Oversew motifs together, placing them as shown in diagram.

Edging

With right side of work facing, join yarn to first corner of 2nd motif on one long side and using 3.50mm hook work 1dc into this loop, *1dc into each tr to next corner, 1dc into corner loop, then 1dc into corner loop of next motif, rep from * to end, working last dc into last corner loop. Turn.

Next row 1ch, (insert hook into next dc and draw a loop through) twice, yarn round hook and draw through all 3 loops on hook – one dc decreased ; decrease 1dc in this way over every 2dc to end of row. Fasten off.

Hood

Darn in all loose ends to wrong side of motifs. Oversew motifs together placing them as shown in diagram, sewing seams A to A and B to B.

Edging

With right side of work facing, join in yarn. Using 3.50mm hook work 1 dc into each tr and loop along lower edge. Fasten off.

To join hood and cape

With right sides together join yarn to corner of first motif on cape and working through the double thickness join the lower edge of the hood to the top edge of the cape by working 1dc into each dc. Fasten off.

Edging

With right side of work facing, join yarn to lower edge at centre back and using 3.00mm hook work *1dc into each tr and 1 dc into each corner loop along lower edge to corner, work 3dc into the corner loop, rep from * to corner at neck edge, work 3dc into corner, continue to work in this way round hood and down other side of cape to centre back ; join with a ss to first dc. Do not turn.

Next row 1 ch, *1 dc into each of next 3dc, 3ch, ss into top of last dc worked – 1 picot formed ; rep from * all round edge of cape and hood, join with a ss to first ch. Fasten off.

☐ Sew a button to left front, 1 motif in from left front neck edge, and use corner sp on first motif on right for buttonhole.

☐ Press lightly on the wrong side using a warm iron over a damp cloth.

Ties

Using 3.50mm hook and yarn double throughout make a ch 42cm long. Fasten off.

☐ Make another tie in the same way.

☐ Sew 1 tie to each side of hood at neck.

More abbreviations to learn

ch	=	chain
dc	=	double crochet
htr	=	half treble
tr	=	treble
dtr	=	double treble
tr tr	=	triple treble
st(s)	=	stitch(es)

These are the abbreviations that you already know ; most refer to special crochet techniques. To keep instructions short and concise, a number of frequently recurring ordinary words are abbreviated to form part of the special crochet shorthand. Below is a list of some of these words in alphabetical order ; they will now appear in the patterns in the crochet courses so you can become familiar with them.

beg	=	beginning
foll	=	following
gr(s)	=	group(s)
rep	=	repeat
sp(s)	=	space(s)
ss	=	slip stitch

Step-by-step course – 18

Making buttonholes

Both horizontal and vertical buttonholes are easy to make – either on the main fabric of your garment or on a separate band which can be sewn on afterwards. Your pattern will tell you how many buttonholes you should make for your garment. Before working the buttonholes, you should measure the length of the button band -- or the edge of your garment on which the buttons will be sewn – and mark the button positions on it, spacing them at equal distances from each other. Using these marks as a guide, you will know precisely where to make each buttonhole when working the buttonhole band.

Our samples were made with a 4.50mm hook and double knitting yarn, and the buttonhole measures approximately 2cm in length. You can vary the size of the buttonhole by using a different thickness of yarn or a different size hook, or by altering the number of stitches or rows in the buttonhole.

Horizontal buttonholes

1 Make 25 chain and work 4 rows in double crochet. When the buttonholes are being worked on the edge of the main fabric, always make sure that you finish the last row – the one before the buttonhole row – at the centre front edge.

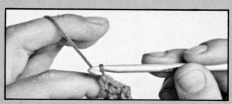

2 Turn and work 3 double crochet. Do not forget to count the turning chain as one stitch. The number of stitches worked at the edge of the fabric will depend on the thickness of yarn being used.

3 Now work 4 chain for the first buttonhole.

4 Miss the next 4 double crochet. Now work 1 double crochet into the next stitch. You can alter the number of chain made and stitches missed in the row below according to the size of buttonhole required.

5 Now work in pattern to the end of the row. Turn and work back to the point where the buttonhole has been made.

6 Work a double crochet into the stitch just before the chain made in the previous row.

7 Now work 1 double crochet into each chain made in the previous row, placing the hook through the middle of the chain each time. This completes the buttonhole.

8 Now work in pattern to the end of the row. The two buttonhole rows are now completed ; there should be the same number of stitches in the row as there were before you worked the hole.

9 Repeat these two rows each time a buttonhole is to be made. If you are making a separate buttonhole band, work the buttonholes in exactly the same way.

Fred Mancini

Vertical buttonholes

1 For this sample we have used a 4.50mm hook and double knitting yarn. Make 17 chain and work 4 rows in double crochet. When working on the main fabric make sure that you always finish the last row – the one before the buttonhole row – at the centre front edge.

2 Turn and work 4 double crochet. Do not forget to count the turning chain as one stitch. Now turn and leave the remaining stitches unworked.

3 Work 6 more rows on these 4 stitches for the first side of the buttonhole, so that you finish the last row at the buttonhole edge.

4 Do not turn. Work in slip stitch down the side of the buttonhole. Work the last slip stitch into the same place as the first double crochet worked for the first side of the buttonhole.

5 Make 1 chain. Now miss 1 stitch and work 1 double crochet into each stitch to the end. Work the last double crochet into the turning chain.

6 Now work 6 more rows on these 12 stitches so that this side has the same number of rows as the other side of the buttonhole. You should finish this row at the side edge of your fabric.

7 Turn and work back to the edge of the buttonhole. Now work 1 double crochet into the edge stitch on the other side of the buttonhole to join the two sides together.

8 Work in pattern to the end of the row to complete the first buttonhole. It is a good idea to count the stitches at this stage to make sure that you have the correct number.

9 Make all the buttonholes in the same way, whether working up the side edge of your fabric, or making a separate band which is to be sewn on afterwards.

Chain button loops

On some crochet fabrics it is not always necessary to make buttonholes since the spaces between the stitches can be used in place of buttonholes. The tiny buttons used on baby clothes can often be fastened through the fabric. However, if you are working an edging round a garment the depth of the edging may prevent your using the fabric in this way. In this case the simplest way to make a buttonhole is to work crochet loops at evenly spaced intervals down the side of your garment.

1 Work a row of double crochet down the side of the garment. Your pattern will tell you the stitch you should use and precisely how many rows to work before you make a button loop.

2 On the edge of the garment mark the positions of the loops by counting the stitches to be worked between loops.

3 Work in double crochet to the point where the first button loop is to be made.

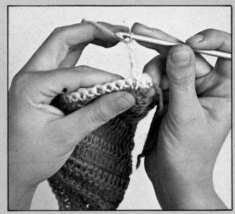

4 Now work 3 chain. You can alter the number of chain to make different sized button loops.

5 Miss the next 3 stitches on the previous row, and work 1 double crochet into the next stitch. The number of stitches you miss should always be the same as the number of chain you have just made.

6 Work in double crochet until you reach the marker for the next loop.

7 Now repeat steps 4 and 5 once more to make the second button loop.

8 Continue down the side of the fabric, working the loops in the same way until the edging is completed.

Fred Mancini

Simple crochet rib

Here is a simple form of ribbing, similar in appearance to knitted fisherman's rib, especially when worked in a chunky yarn. Although it does not have the same degree of elasticity as a knitted rib, it is still very useful for making collars, cuffs and welts. Used for the main fabric of a garment, the stitch makes a really attractive texture which is quick and easy to work.

The method of working differs from the usual way, in that the number of stitches needed to begin the pattern will correspond to the depth of the ribbing required, rather than the width. This means that you are, in effect, working from side to side, rather than from the lower edge to the top, so that it is only when the fabric thus made is turned sideways that the ribbed effect becomes apparent. You work round the garment, rather than starting at lower edge.

Try our sample using a chunky yarn and a 6.00mm hook.

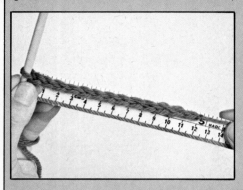

1 Make 13 chain for a piece of ribbing measuring approximately 12cm in depth.

2 Work 1 double crochet into 3rd chain from hook and then 1 double crochet into each chain to the end.

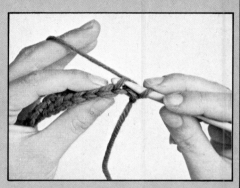

3 Turn 1ch. Miss the first double crochet. Insert the hook from front to back into the back, horizontal loop of the next stitch – not under both loops as in ordinary crochet.

4 Draw the yarn through and complete the double crochet in the normal way.

5 Continue to work a double crochet into each stitch, through the back loop only, in the same way, until only turning chain remains.

6 Work the last stitch into the back of the turning chain. If you work into the turning chain in the normal way you will find that the edge of your work becomes distorted.

7 Work each row in the same way until the piece is the required length. This should be the same length as the width of the garment you are making.

8 When the ribbing is to be used as a welt or cuff, turn the work at the end of the last row so that the rows just worked now run vertically rather than horizontally.

9 Continue to work along the side edge of the ribbing to begin the main part of the garment, working one stitch into each row end unless your instructions tell you otherwise.

Fred Mancini

82

Final list of abbreviations

beg = beginning		alt = alternate
ch = chain		cont = continu(e) (ing)
dc = double crochet		dec = decreas(e) (ing)
dtr = double treble		inc = increas(e) (ing)
foll = following		patt = pattern
gr(s) = group(s)		rem = remain(ing)
htr = half treble		RS = right side
rep = repeat		tog = together
sp(s) = space(s)		WS = wrong side
ss = slip stitch		yrh = yarn round hook
st(s) = stitch(es)		
tr = treble		
tr tr = triple treble		

The list on the left gives, alphabetically, the abbreviations you have learned so far. To complete your knowledge of crochet shorthand, we list the remaining commonly-used terms, along with their abbreviations. There are a few more crochet abbreviations for specialized terms, which will be introduced as they arise in the course. From now on, the course patterns will use all the standard abbreviations.

Shetland waistcoat

For keeping the winter chill out this waistcoat is ideal. It's made of warm Shetland wool in an easy-to-work pattern and trimmed with crochet ribbing.

Sizes
To fit 97[102 :107]cm chest.
Length, 61 [63 :65]cm.
Note Instructions for larger sizes are in square brackets [ ]; where there is only one set of figures it applies to all sizes.

Materials
*10[11 :11] x 25g balls of Templetons
   H & O Shetland Fleece
3.50mm crochet hook
4.00mm crochet hook
5 buttons*

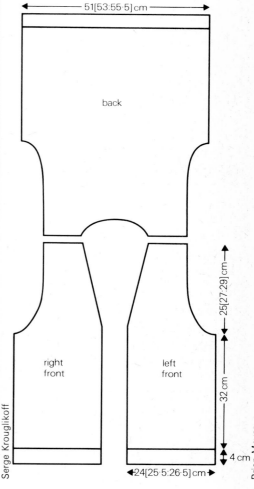

Serge Krouglikoff

Brian Mayor

Tension

18 sts and 20 rows to 10cm over patt worked on a 4.00mm hook.

Back

Using 3.50mm hook make 9ch for side edge of welt.

Base row 1dc into 3rd ch from hook, 1dc into each ch to end. Turn. 8sts. Commence rib.

Rib row 2ch to count as first dc, * 1dc into back loop only of next st, rep from * to end. Work last dc into back loop of turning chain. Turn.

Rep the last row 89[93:97] times more. This completes ribbing for welt. Do not turn. Work along one long edge.

Next row 1ch, now work 1dc into each row end all along this edge. Turn. Commence patt.

Next row 2ch, miss first st, * miss next dc, work 2dc into next dc, rep from * to end. Turn.

This row forms the patt and is repeated throughout. Cont in patt until work measures 36cm from beg.

Shape armholes

Decrease 2sts at each end of next 2 rows, then one st at each end of next 6 rows. 72[76:80]sts. Cont without shaping until armhole measures 25[27:29]cm from beg.

Shape shoulders and neck

Next row Ss over first 5sts, 2ch to count as first st, now work in patt over first 16[17:18]sts (remember to count the first 2ch as one st). Turn. Complete the right shoulder on these sts.

Next row Decrease one st, patt to last 5sts. Turn. Draw yarn through and fasten off.

Return to remaining sts. With RS of work facing, miss next 30[32:34]sts, rejoin yarn to next st, 2ch, now work in patt to last 5sts, turn and leave these sts unworked.

Next row Ss over first 5sts, work in patt to last 2sts, work these 2sts together to decrease one st. Draw yarn through and fasten off.

Left front

Using 3.50mm hook make 9ch. Work

base row and rib row as given for back. Rep rib row 41[43:45] times more. Do not turn but work along one long edge of welt as given for back. 44[46:48]sts. Change to 4.00mm hook. Cont in patt as given for back until work measures same as back to armhole, ending at side edge.

Shape armhole and front edge

1st row Ss over first 2sts, 2ch, patt to last 2sts, work these 2sts together to decrease one st. Turn.

2nd row Work in patt to last 2sts. Turn.

Dec one st at armhole edge on next 6 rows, and *at the same time* decrease one st at front edge on every 3rd row until 20[21:22]sts rem. Cont without shaping until armhole measures same as back to shoulder, ending at armhole edge.

Shape shoulder

Next row Ss over first 5sts, 2ch, work in patt to end of row. Turn.

Next row Patt to last 5sts, turn and leave these sts unworked.

Draw yarn through and fasten off.

Right front

Work as given for left front, but reversing shaping so that armhole and neck shaping are worked on the opposite side to left front.

Front border

Join shoulder seams on WS, using a back stitch seam. Using 3.50mm hook and with RS of right front facing, work a row of dc up right front, round neck and down left front, working 1dc into each row end. Work 7 rows in rib as given for back, making 5 buttonholes on 4th row, the first to come approximately 1.5cm from the lower edge, with 4 more evenly spaced up left front at approximately 7.5cm intervals as follows :

Work to point where first buttonhole is to be made, make 3ch and miss the next 3dc, cont in patt to the position for the next buttonhole, and work another one in the same way. The last buttonhole should be worked at the point where the front neck shaping begins. On the next row, work 1dc into each of the 3ch made in the previous row to complete the buttonhole. Draw yarn through and fasten off.

Armhole borders

Work as given for front border for 5 rows, omitting buttonholes.

To make up

Press work lightly under a damp cloth with a warm iron if necessary, omitting ribbing. Join side seams using back stitch seam. Press seams lightly. Sew on buttons to correspond with buttonholes.

Serge Krouglikoff

Step-by-step course – 19

Crochet edgings

Crochet edgings are extremely versatile, giving you plenty of scope for adding your individual touch to the garment you are making.

In this course we show you how to work a selection of different edgings directly on to your fabric. These edgings can be used simply to neaten the edge of the fabric (for example, a plain crab stitch edging on a really chunky garment) or for decorative effect as well (for example, a delicate chain loop edge round a baby's shawl). The edgings may be worked on to crocheted or knitted fabric, using the same or a contrasting coloured yarn. It is important, however, to choose a type of yarn and edging appropriate to the garment you have made. Use a fine edging to go round a baby's dress or summer top and a heavier edging for a chunky jacket or coat.

If you are working down the side of your fabric, rather than into each stitch across the row, you may need first to work a row of double crochet to form a firm base for the edging. The number of double crochet you work down the row ends depends on the kind of stitch, hook and yarn used for the main fabric. Make sure you do not work too few stitches, as this pulls the edge and distorts the shape.

Crab stitch edging

This popular and very simple edging is an ideal way to give a firm neat edge to a chunky garment. The finished result is not unlike a form of blanket stitching, and for this reason it is particularly effective when worked in a chunky yarn on a thick fabric.

1 Work 1 row of double crochet as a base row along the edge of your fabric. Work the last double crochet into the corner of the fabric.

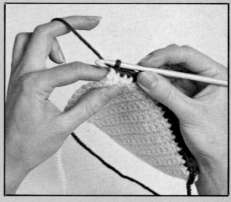

2 Do not turn the work as you would normally do. Keep holding the yarn and hook in the same hands as before, with the yarn to the left of the work.

3 You now continue to work back along the row from left to right, rather than from right to left in the usual way. Begin by making 1 chain.

4 Miss the first stitch and insert the hook from front to back into the next stitch. Now place the hook over the yarn.

5 Draw the yarn through and complete the double crochet in the usual way. Work 1 double crochet into each stitch along the row in the same way. Fasten off.

Fred Mancini

Lace shell edging

This pretty lace edging looks best in a 4 ply or finer yarn. We show you how to work down the side of the garment, but you can, of course, work across the fabric, working into each stitch rather than each row end.

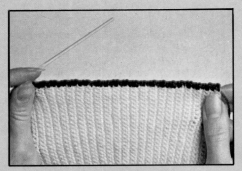

1 Work a row of double crochet along the edge of your fabric as a base row for the edging. This will also help to neaten the edge of your fabric.

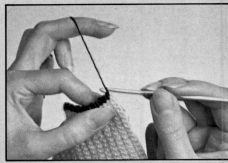

2 Turn the work so that you are ready to work back along the double crochet row in the normal way. Now make 1 chain, miss the first 2 double crochet.

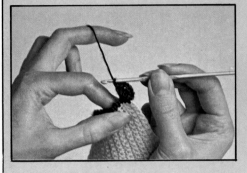

3 Work 2 treble, then 2 chain and 2 treble all into the next double crochet. Miss the next 2 double crochet.

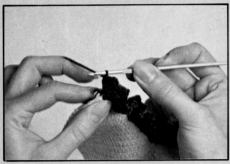

4 Repeat step 3 all along the edge of the fabric until only one double crochet remains unworked.

5 Complete the edging by working a slip stitch into the corner of the fabric. Fasten off.

Scalloped shell edging

This edging is most effective when worked directly on to the fabric, rather than over a base of double crochet. It can either be worked into the stitches across the row or into the row ends and produces a scalloped effect on the edge of your garment.

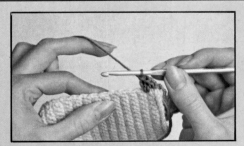

1 Join yarn to corner. Make one chain. Miss the next row end (or stitch) and work 3 treble into the following row end to form the first shell shape.

2 Now miss the next row end and work 1 double crochet into the following row end.

3 Miss the next row end and work 3 treble into the following row end for the 2nd shell.

4 Continue to repeat steps 2 and 3 all the way across the edge until the last shell has been worked.

5 Now miss the next row end and work the last double crochet into the corner of the fabric. Fasten off.

Chain loop edging

The pretty arched effect of this simple lace edging is achieved by working a series of chain loops on top of each other. You could make the edging deeper by working more chain loops until it is the depth you require.

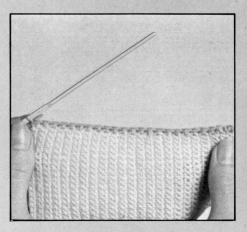

1 Work a base row of double crochet down the side of the fabric. Make sure that you work an even number of stitches for this edging.

2 Turn and work 1 chain to count as the first double crochet. Now work 5 more chain. Miss the next double crochet and work 1 double crochet into the next stitch, thus forming the first arch.

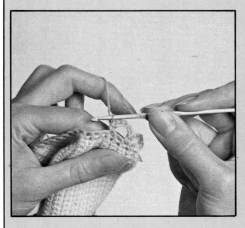

3 Work 5 chain. Miss the next double crochet and work 1 double crochet into the next stitch for the second arch.

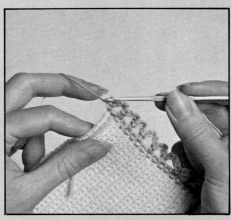

4 Repeat step 3 all the way along the row, working the last double crochet into the corner of your fabric.

5 Turn the work. Now make 5 chain and then 1 double crochet into the centre of the first 5 chain loop of the previous row.

6 Make 5 chain. Now work 1 double crochet into the centre of the next 5 chain loop.

7 Continue to repeat step 6 all along the row until only 1 loop remains unworked in the previous row.

8 Work 5 chain as before. Now work a slip stitch instead of a double crochet into the centre of the last loop and fasten off the yarn.

Fred Mancini

Young Victoriana

For those special occasions, this apron will brighten up a plain dress. It is worked in a simple stitch and edged with shells around the straps and skirt.

Sizes
To suit 56[61:66]cm chest.
Length from shoulder, 47 [52:57]cm.

Note Instructions for larger sizes are in square brackets []. Where there is only one set of figures it applies to all sizes.

Materials
6[7:8] balls of Robin Suzette Crochet Courtelle
3.00mm crochet hook
2 buttons

Tension
22 sts and 22 rows to 10cm over patt worked on a 3.00mm hook.

Skirt
Using 3.00mm hook make 58 [64:70]ch.
Base row Work 1dc into 4th ch from hook, * now work 1tr into next ch, 1dc into next ch, rep from * to end. Turn. 56[62:68] sts.

Patt row 3ch to count as first tr, miss first dc, * work 1dc into next tr, 1tr into next dc, rep from * to end of row. Work last dc into turning ch, turn. The last row forms the patt and is repeated throughout. Cont in patt until work measures 24 [27:30]cm from beg.

Work edging
Do not turn work, but continue to work down side edge, working 1dc into each row end to lower edge, 1dc into rem loop of each ch along lower edge and 1dc into each row end up other side of work. Fasten off. With RS of work facing rejoin yarn to beg of edging and work 1ch, * miss next dc, work 2tr. 2ch and 2tr all into next dc to make a shell, miss next dc, 1dc into next dc, rep from * round 3 sides as before.
Fasten off.

Bib
Using 3.00mm hook make 30 [34:38]ch. Work base row and patt row as given for skirt. 28[32:36] sts. Cont in patt until bib measures 12[13:14] cm from beg.

Work straps
Patt over first 6 [6:8] sts, turn and leave rem sts unworked. Cont on these sts for 30 [32:34]cm. Fasten off.
Return to rem sts. Miss next 16[20:20] sts, rejoin yarn to next st and work in patt to end of row.
Complete as given for first strap.

Edging
Work edging as given for skirt along outer edges of bib and straps, and then along inner edge of 1st strap, across top of bib and along inner edge of 2nd strap. Fasten off.

Waistband and ties
Using 3.00mm hook make 9ch. Work 1dc into 3rd ch from hook, 1dc into each ch to end. Turn. 8 sts. Cont to work in dc until band measures 95 [100:105] cm from beg. Fasten off.

Pocket
Using 3.00mm hook make 18 [22:26] ch. Work base row and patt row as given for skirt. 16 [20:24] sts. Cont in patt until pocket measures 7 [8:9]cm from beg.
Shape top
Next row 1ch, 1dc into each of next 3 sts, * miss next tr, 1dc into each of next 3 sts, rep from * to end so that only 13 [16:19] sts rem.
Next row 1ch, miss 1 [0:0]dc, * work 2tr, 2ch and 2tr all into next dc, miss next dc, 1dc into next dc, rep from * 1 [2:3] times more, work 2tr, 2ch and 2tr all into next dc, miss 1 [1:0]dc, 1dc into turning ch. Fasten off.

To make up
Press work lightly, if you wish, under a dry cloth with a cool iron. Sew lower edge of bib to centre of waistband. Sew top of skirt to other side of waistband, gathering top slightly. Sew a button 7cm from each side of waistband and make a loop at end of each strap to fasten. Sew on pocket. Press seams.

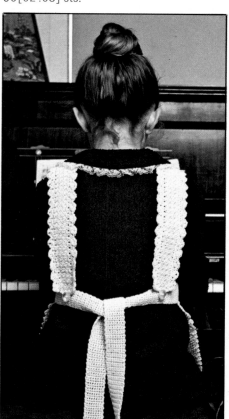

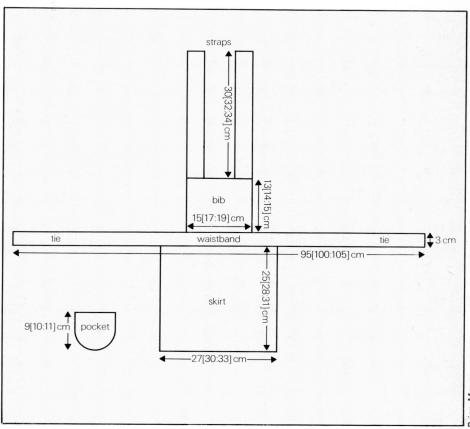

Step-by-step course – 20

An introduction to Aran-style crochet

'Aran' is a term which is rightly associated with knitting, rather than crochet. It refers to the intricate and highly textured knitting stitches that originated on the Aran Islands of Inishmore, Inisheer and Inishmaan, off the West Coast of Ireland.

Although crochet cannot duplicate exactly the appearance of Aran knitting, it can create patterns that resemble some of the Aran stitches, such as moss stitch, berry stitch and many others. This Aran-style crochet has its own appeal, and devotees of crochet appreciate its relative

simplicity, compared to knitting, as well as its pleasing appearance.

The following step-by-step instructions are intended to help you work two of the more complicated stitches used to make the Afghan featured at the end of this course.

Uneven berry stitch

This simple, but effective, stitch is worked by drawing the yarn several times through the same stitch, then working all the loops off the hook to make a bobble or 'berry'. The size of the bobble depends on the number of times the yarn is drawn through the stitch (and also, of course, on the thickness of the yarn). Practise making the bobbles with an Aran-type yarn and a 6.00mm hook. Make 20 chain and start the sample by working 18 double crochet into the chain so that there are 19 stitches in all, including the turning chain.

1 Begin the first row of the pattern with 1 chain. This will be the WS of the work. Miss the first double crochet. Now wind the yarn round the hook and insert it into the next double crochet.

2 Wind the yarn round the hook and draw it through the stitch, pulling up the yarn so that the loop is quite loose.

3 Wind the yarn round the hook and draw it through the first loop on the hook. 3 loops now remain on the hook.

4 Wind the yarn round the hook and insert it once more into the same stitch as before. Repeat step 2 once more. 5 loops on the hook.

5 Wind the yarn round the hook and draw it through the first 4 loops. 2 loops remain. Now draw yarn in same way through last 2 loops to form bobble.

6 Work 1 slip stitch into the next double crochet to hold the bobble in place.

7 Work 1 bobble into next stitch, then 1 slip stitch into the next stitch, alternately until 2 stitches remain.

8 Work 1 bobble into the next stitch and then 1 double crochet into the turning chain to complete the first row.

continued

Fred Mancini

Continued : uneven berry stitch

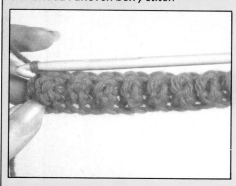

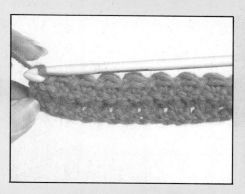

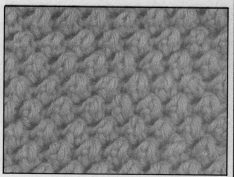

9 Turn. The 2nd row is worked on the RS of the work. Make 1 chain and miss the first double crochet. Now work a slip stitch into the top of each bobble and 1 double crochet into each slip stitch across the row. Work the last double crochet into the turning chain.

10 The 3rd row is worked like the first, but to alter the position of the bobbles, you must work 1 slip stitch into each slip stitch and 1 bobble into each double crochet of the previous row.

11 The bobbles are alternated in the same way each time. You work a slip stitch into each berry and a double crochet into each slip stitch on RS rows and a bobble into each double crochet and a slip stitch into each slip stitch on WS rows. Alter the row ends accordingly to keep pattern correct.

Lattice stitch

This highly textured stitch with a lattice or honeycomb effect is achieved by working double trebles on to the front of the fabric, working round the stem of the stitch rather than into the top of the stitches in the normal way. It is important to place the hook correctly, but once you have mastered this technique you will find the pattern quite simple to work. The step-by-step instructions show you exactly how this is done.

To work the sample make 22 chain, using a chunky or Aran-type yarn, and work 20 trebles into this chain, including the turning chain.

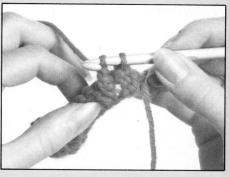

1 Begin to work the pattern on the front of these trebles. Wind yarn twice round the hook and insert hook into base of the 3rd treble, working from right to left so that your hook passes through the stitch.

2 Yarn round hook and draw a loop of yarn through the stitch to give 4 loops on hook. Now wind yarn round hook and draw it through first 2 loops. Repeat this action once more through second 2 loops. This makes 1 open double treble, leaving 2 loops on hook.

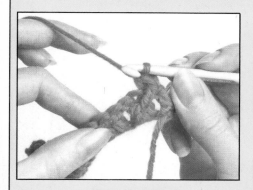

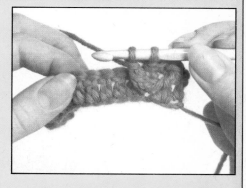

3 Insert the hook into top of the first treble of the row and draw through a loop. 3 loops on hook. Now wind yarn round hook and draw it through these 3 loops. This closes the first open double treble.

4 Work 1 double crochet into each of the next 2 stitches. The first of these stitches should be worked into the stitch behind the double treble.

5 Now work an open double treble as before into the same stitch as the last open double treble, so that you make a V-shape on the front of the fabric.

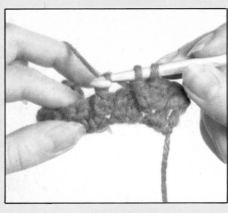

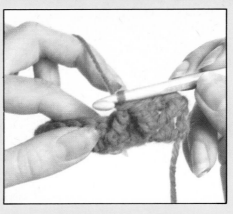

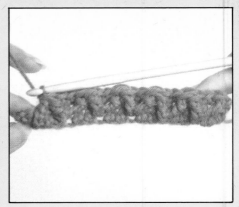

6 Miss the next 2 treble and work another open double treble into the base of the next stitch in the same way as before. 3 loops on hook.

7 Now insert the hook into the first stitch after the last double crochet worked and pull yarn through. Wind yarn round hook and draw it through all 4 loops on hook. This will be called close 2 double treble.

8 Repeat steps 4 to 7 four more times, so that you have worked 11 double trebles on the front of the fabric in all.

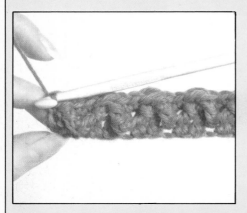

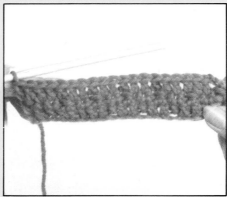

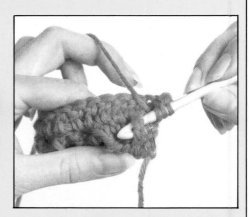

9 Repeat steps 4 and 5 once more. Now insert the hook into the next double crochet and draw a loop through. Now draw yarn through all 3 loops on hook. Work 1 double crochet into the turning chain to complete first row.

10 Turn. Make 3 chain. Now work 1 treble into each stitch to end of row. You should have 20 stitches in all.

11 Turn. Make 1 chain. Miss first stitch and work 1 double crochet into next stitch. Wind yarn twice round hook and insert it from right to left round the back of the first double treble 2 rows below.

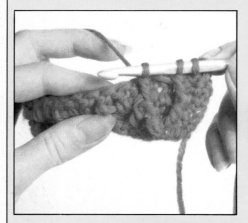

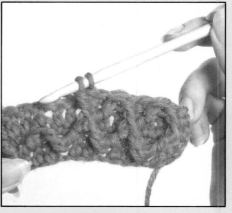

12 Complete the open double treble as before. Now work another open double treble, inserting the hook from right to left behind next group of 2 double treble where they meet at the top.

13 Repeat step 7 once more to close these 2 stitches. Repeat step 4 once more. Work an open double treble round same group as last double treble to make the first V-shape of this row.

14 Work 1 open double treble group round next group. Repeat step 7, then step 4 once more. Work an open double treble round same group as last double treble for next V.

Fred Mancini

continued

Continued : lattice stitch

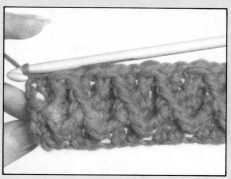

Fred Mancini

15 Continue to work across the row in this way until you have worked 2 open double trebles round last group and only the single double treble in the previous row remains unworked.

16 Work an open double treble round the last remaining double treble. Now repeat step 7 to close these 2 stitches, and work 1 double crochet into each of the last 2 stitches to complete the row.

17 This completed sample shows several rows of this stitch, worked so that you can see the full effect of working double trebles in this way.

Aran-style Afghan

The enduring appeal of Aran patterns — worked here in crochet — will make this Afghan a treasured family heirloom. Four different stitches are used to make the squares, and the completed squares are then joined together.

Size
143cm x 191cm, approx.

Note This Afghan is made up of four different patterned squares. For easy reference we have given them each a letter — A, B, C and D.

Materials
53 x 50g balls of Marriner Regency Aran Bainin
6.00mm and 7.00mm crochet hooks

Tension
A, 4 patt repeats to 6cm in width worked on 7.00mm hook
B, 3 patt repeats to 5cm in width worked on 7.00mm hook
C, 8 dc to 6cm in width worked on 6.00mm hook
D, 2 patt repeats to 5cm in width worked on 6.00mm hook

A (worked in even moss stitch)
Using 7.00mm hook make 31ch fairly loosely.
Base row (RS) Ss into 3rd ch from hook, * 1htr into next ch, ss into next ch, rep from * to end. Turn.
Patt row 2ch to count as first htr, miss first ss, *ss into next htr, 1htr into next ss, rep from * to within turning ch, ss into 2nd of first 2ch. Turn.
Rep the patt row until work measures 23cm from beg. Fasten off.
Make 11 more squares in the same way.

B (worked in uneven berry stitch)
Using 7.00mm hook make 30ch fairly loosely.
Base row (RS) 1dc into 3rd ch from hook, then work 1dc into each ch to end. Turn.
1st row 1ch, miss first dc, *yrh, insert hook into next dc and draw a loop through loosely, yoh and draw through one loop on hook (3 loops on hook), yrh, insert hook into same dc and draw a loop through loosely (5 loops on hook), yrh and draw through 4 loops on hook, yrh and draw through rem 2 loops on hook — called B1, ss into next dc, rep from * to last 2 sts, B1 into next dc, 1dc into 2nd of first 2ch. Turn.
2nd row 1ch, miss first dc, *ss into next B1, 1dc into next ss, rep from * to within last 2 sts, ss into next B1, 1dc into first ch. Turn.
3rd row 1ch, miss first dc, *ss into next ss, B1 into next dc, rep from * to within last 2 sts, ss into next ss, 1dc into first ch. Turn.
4th row 1ch, miss first dc, *1dc into next ss, ss into next B1, rep from * to within last 2 sts, 1dc into next ss, 1dc into first ch. Turn.
5th row 1ch, miss first dc, *B1 into next dc, ss into next ss, rep from * to within last 2 sts, B1 into next dc, 1dc into first ch. Turn.
The 2nd to 5th rows form the patt.
Cont in patt until work measures 23cm from beg, ending with 2nd or 4th row. Fasten off.
Make 11 more squares in the same way.

C (worked in rib)
Using 6.00mm hook make 32ch fairly loosely.
Base row (WS) 1dc into 3rd ch from hook, 1dc into each ch to end. Turn.
Patt row 1ch to count as first dc, miss first dc, 1dc into each dc to end, placing the hook into the horizontal loop under the normal ch loop of the dc, 1dc into turning ch, turn.
Rep the patt row until work measures 23cm from beg. Fasten off.
Make 11 more squares in the same way.

D (worked in lattice stitch)
Using 6.00mm hook make 29ch fairly loosely.
Base row (WS) 1tr into 3rd ch from hook, 1tr into each ch to end, turn.
1st row Working patt on front of the fabric work (yrh) twice, insert hook into base of 3rd tr on base row from right to left, yrh and draw a loop through, (yrh and draw through 2 loops on hook) twice — called 1 open dtr, insert hook into top of first tr, yrh and draw a loop through, yrh and draw through all 3 loops on hook — called close 1 dtr, 1dc in each of next 2tr, * 1 open dtr into base of same tr as before, miss next 2 tr, 1 open dtr in base of next tr, insert hook into top of tr after last dc worked, yrh and draw a loop through, yrh and draw through all 4 loops on hook — called close 2dtr, 1dc into each of next 2tr, rep from * to within last tr, 1 open dtr into base of same tr as before, close 1 dtr in last tr. Turn.
2nd row 2ch for first tr, miss first dc, 1tr into each dc to end. Turn. 28tr.
3rd row 1 ch for first dc, miss first tr, 1dc into next tr, inserting hook from right to left under first dtr 2 rows below, work 1 open dtr, then work 1 open dtr

under next gr of 2dtr, close 2dtr, 1dc
in each of next 2tr, * 1 open dtr under
same gr of 2dtr as before, 1 open dtr
under next gr of 2dtr, close 2dtr, 1dc
into each of next 2tr, rep from * to
within last 2tr, 1 open dtr, under same
gr of 2dtr as before, 1 open dtr under
last dtr, close 2dtr, 1dc into last tr. Turn.
4th row As 2nd patt row.
5th row 1 open dtr under first gr of
2 dtr, close 1dtr working into first tr,
1dc into each of next 2tr, * 1 open dtr
under same gr of 2dtr as before, 1 open
dtr into next gr of 2dtr, close 2dtr,
1 dc into each of next 2tr, rep from * to
within last tr, 1 open dtr under same gr
of 2dtr as before, 1 open dtr into last
tr, close 2 dtr. Turn.
The 2nd to 5th rows form the patt.
Cont to rep these rows until work
measures 23cm from beg, ending with a
5th row. Fasten off.
Make 11 more squares in the same way.

To make up
Join the squares tog with a flat seam
on the WS of the work, following the
diagram.

Border
With RS facing and using 7.00mm hook
join yarn to one corner and make 1ch
to count as first dc, work an uneven
number of dc evenly along each edge
with 3dc into the first 3 corners and 2dc
into last corner join with ss to first ch.
Turn. Work in uneven moss stitch as foll :
1st round Ss into centre dc at first corner,
1ch to count as first dc, * (ss into next
dc, 1htr into next dc) to centre dc at next
corner, 3dc into centre dc, rep from * all
round edge ending with a ss into first ss,
2 dc into same dc as ss, ss into first ch to
complete the round. Turn.
2nd round Ss into centre dc at first
corner, 1ch for first dc, * (1htr into next
dc, ss into ss, 1htr into next htr, ss into
next ss), to 3dc at next corner, 1htr into
next dc, 3dc into next dc, rep from * all
round edge ending last rep with 1htr into
first ss, 2dc into same dc as ss, ss into first
ch to complete the round. Turn.
3rd round Ss into centre dc at first
corner, 1ch, * (1htr into next dc, ss into
next htr, 1htr into next ss, ss into next
htr) to 3dc at next corner, 1htr into next
dc, 3dc into next dc, rep from * all
round edge ending last rep with 1htr
into first ss, 2dc into same dc as ss, ss into
first ch to complete the round. Turn.
4th round Ss into centre dc at first
corner, 1ch, * (ss into next dc, 1htr into
next htr, ss into next ss, 1htr into next
htr) to 3dc at next corner ss into next dc,
3 dc into next dc, rep from * all round
edge ending last rep with ss into first ss.
2dc into same dc as ss, ss into first ch
to complete the round. Turn.
5th round Ss into centre dc at first
corner, 1 ch, * (ss into next dc, 1 htr into

next ss, ss into next htr, 1htr into next
ss) to 3 dc at next corner, ss into next dc,
3dc into next dc, rep from * all round
edge, ending last rep with ss into first
ss, 2dc into same dc as ss, ss to first ch
to complete the round. Turn.

Rep the 2nd, 3rd and 4th rounds once
more.
Fasten off.
Press work lightly on the wrong side
with a warm iron and a damp cloth, taking
care not to flatten the pattern.

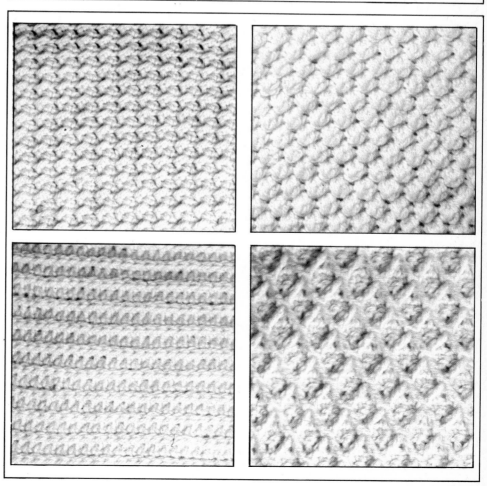

John Hutchinson

C	B	A	D	C	B	A	D
D	C	B	A	D	C	B	A
A	D	C	B	A	D	C	B
B	A	D	C	B	A	D	C
C	B	A	D	C	B	A	D
D	C	B	A	D	C	B	A

143 cm

191 cm

Step-by-step course – 21

More about Aran-style crochet

In the previous course we showed you how to work some of the background stitches which can be used in crochet to produce Aran-type fabrics. Here we concentrate on how to work cables and zig-zag patterns by working round the stem of certain stitches to produce a raised effect. Double crochet, half trebles or crochet moss stitch are the best stitches to use for the background, since they make a firm, even fabric. Treble and double treble fabrics tend to be too open and therefore the motifs will not stand out so effectively against them. Once you have practised our samples, you will find it quite easy to experiment with the basic working method. For example, simply by varying the number of rows worked before crossing a cable each time, you can alter its appearance considerably. Similarly, by working three or four stitches together in the zig-zag pattern, rather than separating the stitches each time, you will produce quite a different effect.

Simple zig-zag pattern

This pattern shows you how raised trebles can be made to slant alternately from right to left to produce a zig-zag effect. You can vary the pattern, either by working two or more raised stitches side by side for a more solid effect, or by working a stitch between each raised treble as shown here.

To make this sample use a chunky or Aran type yarn and a 5.50mm hook. Make 24 chain and work 23 double crochet into the chain (including the turning chain).

1 Begin the next row with 1 chain. Miss the first double crochet and work 1 double crochet into the next stitch. Miss the next double crochet and work 1 treble into the next stitch.

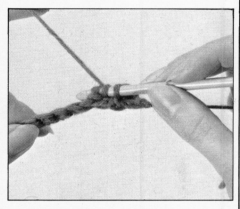

2 Keep the hook at the back of the work so that it is behind the treble just made. Wind the yarn round the hook and insert it from front to back through the stitch just missed.

3 Now complete this treble in the usual way. These 2 treble have been crossed at the back of the work.

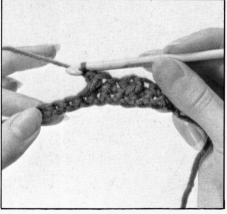

4 Work 1 double crochet into the next stitch and then cross the next 2 stitches at the back in the same way as before. This completes the first group of crossed trebles.

5 Work 1 double crochet into each of the next 2 double crochet. Now cross the next 2 trebles at the back of the work as before.

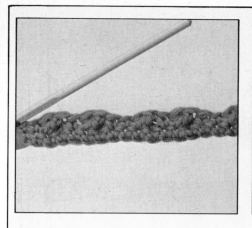

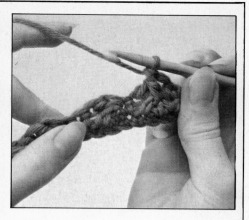

6 Continue to repeat steps 4 and 5 all the way across row, ending with step 4. Work 1 double crochet into the next stitch, then 1 double crochet into the turning chain. There should be 3 groups of 2 crossed trebles in all.

7 Turn. Make 1 chain. Miss the first stitch and work 1 double crochet into the next stitch. Miss next treble. Work 1 treble into next treble. Keep the hook at the front of the work. Wind yarn round hook and insert it from right to left round stem of missed raised treble.

8 Complete this treble in the usual way. These 2 trebles have now been crossed at the front (RS) of the fabric. Work crossed trebles at front in the same way each time.

9 Work 1 double crochet into the next double crochet. Now cross the next 2 trebles at front (RS) of fabric as before.

10 Continue to work across the row in this way, with 1 double crochet worked into each double crochet and 2 trebles crossed at the front each time. Work last double crochet into the turning chain.

11 Turn. Now work 1 chain and first 2 stitches as in step 7. Keep hook at back (RS) of work. Wind yarn round hook and place hook round stem of missed raised treble on RS of work from right to left.

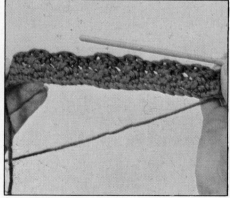

12 Wind yarn round hook and complete the treble in the normal way. This crosses the 2 trebles at back and slants them to the right on RS of fabric.

13 Continue to work 1 double crochet into each double crochet and cross two trebles at back (RS) of work each time. Work last double crochet into turning chain. Here we show you the completed row on the RS.

14 Each row is worked alternately to make the pattern, so that the trebles are crossed at the front when the RS is facing and at the back when the WS is facing.

Mike Berend

Mock cable panel

Here we show you how to work a cable on a half treble background. We use the same basic principle of working round the stem of the stitches in the row below to produce a raised effect. By using double trebles to cross the stitches you can achieve a cable effect, and you can vary the appearance of the cables simply by working fewer or more rows between each cross-over row.

To make this sample, first make 14 chain and work 13 half treble into the chain. We have used a 5.50mm hook and Aran type yarn.

1 Turn. Make 2 chain. Now work 1 half treble into each of next 3 stitches. Begin each cable row in the same way. Now wind the yarn round the hook and insert it round the stem of the next stitch from right to left.

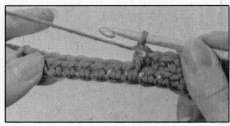

2 Now complete 1 treble in the usual way. This completes the first raised treble. Work each raised treble in the same way.

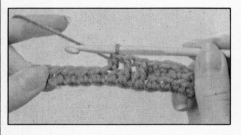

3 Work another raised treble round the stem of the next stitch. Now work 1 half treble into the next half treble. This stitch is in the centre of the cable and separates the raised stitches.

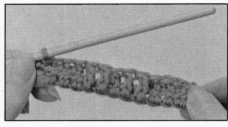

4 Work 1 raised treble round the stem of each of the next 2 stitches. Now work 1 half treble into each stitch to the end of the row (4 in all). Complete each cable row in this way.

5 Begin the 2nd pattern row with 1 chain. Miss the first stitch and work 1 half treble into each stitch to the end so that there are 13 stitches. Work each alternate row in the same way.

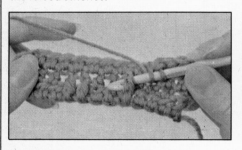

6 Turn and begin cable row as before. Now wind the yarn round the hook and insert it from right to left round the raised treble worked in the previous cable row.

7 Complete the treble as before extending the yarn slightly to avoid distorting the fabric. Work another raised treble round the next raised treble in the previous cable row. Now work 1 half treble into the next (centre) half treble.

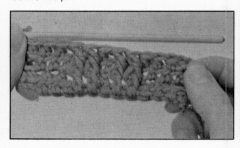

8 Work 1 raised treble round each of the next 2 raised trebles in the previous cable row. This completes the cable section for this row. Complete the row as before.

9 Turn and repeat step 5 once more. Now turn and work 4 half treble as before for the beginning of the next row.

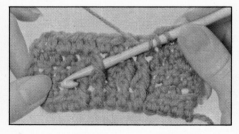

10 Miss the next 2 raised trebles in the previous row and the centre half treble. Wind yarn twice round hook and insert hook from right to left round next raised treble.

11 Complete 1 double treble in the normal way. Work another raised double treble round the next raised treble in the previous row. These 2 stitches now slant to the right.

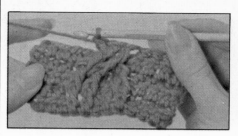

Mike Berend

12 Hold the hook behind these 2 stitches and work 1 half treble into the missed (centre) half treble. Still keeping the hook behind the 2 double trebles, work 1 double treble round the first of the missed raised trebles.

13 Work another double treble in the same way round the 2nd of missed raised trebles. These 2 stitches slant from right to left behind first 2 double trebles.

14 Complete the row as before. Work the next cable twist by repeating steps 5 to 8 twice. Now repeat steps 9 to 13 once more. You have thus worked 5 rows in all before crossing the raised trebles again.

Stitch Wise

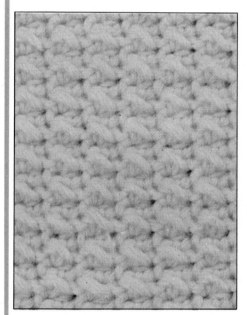

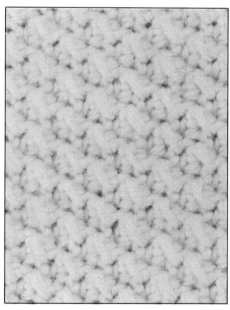

Even moss stitch
Make a length of chain which has a multiple of 2 stitches.
1st row Miss first ch, ss into next ch, *1 htr into next ch, ss into next ch, rep from * to end. Turn.
2nd row 1 ch, miss first st, *1 htr into next st, ss into next st, rep from * to end of row, working last ss into turning chain. Turn. The 2nd row forms the patt. Repeat it each time.

Uneven moss stitch
Make a length of chain which has a multiple of 2 stitches.
Work the 1st and 2nd rows in exactly the same way as given for even moss stitch.
3rd row 2ch to count as first htr, miss first st, ss into next st, *1 htr into next st, ss into next st, rep from * to end of row, working last htr into turning chain. Turn.
4th row As 3rd.
5th row As 2nd row.
6th row As 2nd row.
The 3rd to 6th rows form the pattern and are repeated throughout.

Aran rib stitch
Make a length of chain with a multiple of 2 plus 1 extra chain.
1st row (RS of fabric) Work 1 htr into 3rd ch from hook, 1 htr into each ch to end. Turn.
2nd row 2ch, miss first st, *work 1 htr into horizontal loop (below two horizontal loops at top of stitch) at front of next htr, rep from * to end, working last htr into turning chain. Turn.
3rd row 2ch, miss first st, *work 1 htr into back loop of top two horizontal loops of next st, rep from * to end, working last htr into turning chain. Turn. 2nd and 3rd rows form patt and are repeated throughout.
This stitch gives the appearance of rib, although the WS of the fabric is flat.

Artful Aran

The intriguing textures of Aran-style crochet are used here to make a smart pullover for a child. The round neckline goes easily over a shirt and the saddle shoulders add extra style.

Sizes
To fit 66[71 :76]cm chest.
Length, 42[46 :50]cm.
Sleeve seam, 33[36 :39]cm.
Note Instructions for larger sizes are in square brackets [] ; where there is only one set of figures it applies to all sizes.

Materials
17[19 :21] x 20g balls of Robin Reward Double Knitting or 15[17 :19] x 20g balls of Robin Reward Double Knitting and 2 balls in a contrasting colour
3.50mm and 4.00mm crochet hooks

Tension
18 sts and 18 rows to 10cm over moss stitch on 4.00mm hook.

Front and back (alike)
Using 3.50mm hook make 9[10 :11] ch for side edge of welt.
Base row 1dc into 3rd ch from hook, 1dc into each ch to end. Turn.
Rib row 1ch, 1dc into back loop only of each dc to end. Turn.
Rep the rib row 57[67 :73] times more. This completes ribbing for the welt. Do not turn but work along one long edge.

Next row 2ch to count as first dc, then 1dc into each row end to end. Turn. 59[69 :75] dc.
Change to 4.00mm hook.
Next row (WS) 2ch to count as first htr, *ss into next dc, 1htr into next dc, rep from * to end, finishing ss into turning ch. Turn. Commence moss st patt.
Patt row 2ch, *ss into next htr, 1htr into next ss, rep from * to end, finishing ss into turning ch. Turn. This row forms the patt.
Cont until work measures 39[42 :46]cm, ending with WS row. Fasten off.

Sleeves
Using 3.50mm hook make 8ch for side edge of cuff and work in rib as given for front until 29[33 :39] rows in all have been worked, then work 1dc into each row end along one long side. Turn. 29[33 :39] sts. Change to 4.00mm hook.
1st row 2ch, (ss into next dc, 1htr into next dc) 3[4 :4] times, 1dc into next dc, (miss next dc, 1tr into next dc, keeping hook at back of work, work 1tr into last dc missed, so forming 2 crossed tr, 1dc into next dc) 1[1 :2] times, (yrh, insert hook into next dc, yrh and draw a loop through, yrh and draw through one

loop on hook, yrh, insert hook into same dc, yrh and draw a loop through so having 5 loops on hook, yrh and draw through first 4 loops on hook, yrh and draw through rem 2 loops, called bobble 1, or B1, ss into next dc) 3 times, B1, (1dc into next dc, cross 2 tr) 1[1 :2] times, 1dc into next dc, ss into next dc, (1htr into next dc, ss into next dc) 3[4 :4] times. Turn.
2nd row 2ch, moss st 6[8 :8], 1dc into next dc, (miss next tr, 1tr into next tr, keeping hook at front of work, work 1tr round the tr that was missed, called cross 2tr front, or Cr2F, 1dc into next dc) 1[1 :2] times, (1dc into B1, 1dc into next ss) 3 times, 1dc into B1, (1dc into next dc, Cr2F) 1[1 :2] times, 1dc into next dc, moss st to end. Turn.
3rd row 2ch, moss st 6[8 :8], 1dc into next dc, (miss next tr, 1tr into next tr, keeping hook at back of work, work 1tr round tr that was missed, called cross 2tr back, or Cr2B, 1dc into next dc) 1[1 :2] times, ss into next dc, (B1 into next dc, ss into next dc) 3 times, (1dc into next dc, Cr2B) 1[1 :2] times, 1dc into next dc, moss st to end. Turn.
4th row 2ch, moss st 6[8 :8], 1dc into next dc, (Cr2F, 1dc into next dc) 1[1 :2] times, 1dc into next ss, (1dc into next B1, 1dc into next ss) 3 times, (1dc into next dc, Cr2F) 1[1 :2] times, 1dc into next dc, moss st to end. Turn.
5th row 2ch, moss st 6[8 :8], 1dc into next dc, (Cr2B, 1dc into next dc) 1[1 :2] times, B1 into next dc, (ss into next dc, B1 into next dc) 3 times, 1dc into next dc, (Cr2B, 1dc into next dc) 1[1 :2] times, moss st to end. Turn. The 2nd to 5th rows form the patt.
Cont in this pattern, increasing one st at each end of 2nd and every foll 6th row by working 2sts into the first and last sts, working the extra sts into moss st, until there are 47[51 :57] sts. Cont without shaping until sleeve measures 33[36 :39]cm from beg, ending with a WS row. Cut off yarn. With RS facing rejoin yarn to first dc at beg of panel, cont across panel sts only for 10[11 :12]cm for saddle shoulder extension, ending with a WS row. Fasten off.

Neckband
Using 3.50mm hook make 8ch and work in rib as given for front for 36[39 :42]cm. Fasten off.

To make up
Do not press. Sew saddle extensions to shoulder seams on front and back, then sew top of sleeves to sides of back and front. Join side and sleeve seams. Join short ends of neckband, then sew neckband to neck. Press seams lightly with a cool iron over a dry cloth.

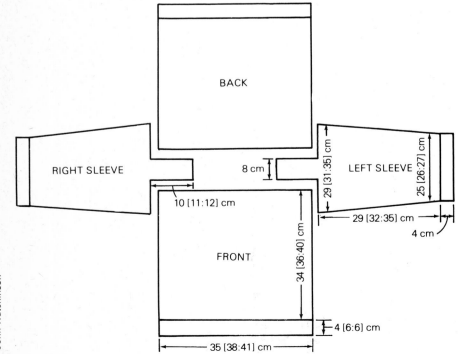

BACK

RIGHT SLEEVE

LEFT SLEEVE

8 cm

29 [31:35] cm

25 [26:27] cm

10 [11:12] cm

29 [32:35] cm

4 cm

FRONT

34 [36:40] cm

4 [6:6] cm

35 [38:41] cm

John Hutchinson

100

Step-by-step course – 22

Basket weave patterns

Once you have mastered the basic crochet stitches and developed a fluent way of working, you'll be amazed at the variety of patterns and stitches you can work – some lacy, others dense and firm. A perfect example of the latter kind of texture is the group of basket weave patterns in this course. Each of them produces a lovely, crunchy fabric with a heavily woven appearance.

Although it looks complicated, the basic basket weave pattern is not difficult to learn. You begin by working a row of trebles; then on the following row you work round the *stem* of the next stitch, rather than under the top two loops as you would normally do when working a treble fabric. The woven effect is achieved by either working round the back of the stitch – which has the effect of pushing it forward – or round the front of the stitch – the stitch pulling to the back.

Blocks of stitches are usually worked alternately forwards and then backwards across the row, the position being reversed on the following row, so that the stitches at the back are brought forward and vice versa. The number of stitches in each block can vary, depending on the fabric you wish to make.

Working basic basket weave

The best way to discover how the fabric is made is to try it yourself. Start by making our sample, using a double knitting yarn and a 4.50mm hook. Our pattern uses blocks of 3 treble and will therefore need a multiple of 3 chain, plus 2 extra for the turning chain (for the sample, 29 chain in all). If you wish, for example, to work 5 treble in each block, you will need to make a multiple of 5 chain plus 2 extra turning chain.

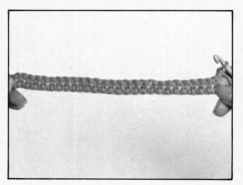

1 Work 1 row of treble (27 in all). Now turn and make 2 chain. Since you are working round the stem below the top of the stitch you need only make 2 chain instead of 3 as you would normally do when working a treble fabric.

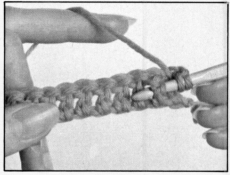

2 Wind the yarn round the hook and insert it round the back of the stem of the 2nd treble, from right to left, taking the hook from the front of the work, through to the back and out to the front again, between the 2nd and 3rd trebles.

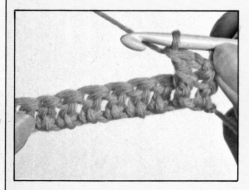

3 Wind the yarn round the hook, draw it through and complete the treble in the normal way. You will see that this treble has been pulled forwards to the front of the fabric.

4 Now work 1 treble round the back of the next treble in the same way to bring the next stitch forward. Including the first 2 chain, 3 stitches have now been worked to the front, making a vertical section. This stitch is called 'treble round front'.

5 Now begin the horizontal part of the pattern. Wind yarn round the hook, insert it from the back of the work, through to the front, round the stem of the next stitch to the left and through to the back of the work again.

Fred Mancini

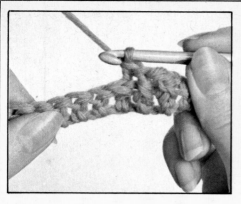

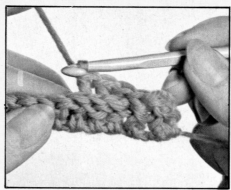

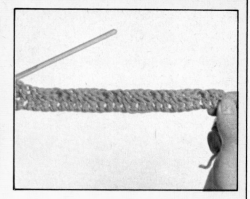

6 Now wind the yarn round the hook, draw it through the stitch, and complete the treble in the normal way, so pulling this treble to the back of the work. This method of working round the front of the stitch to bring it to the back is called 'treble round back'.

7 Work 1 treble in the same way round the front of the stem of each of the next 2 treble, repeating steps 5 and 6 each time. Keep the hook at the back of the work while working these trebles.

8 Work the next 3 treble to the front as before, repeating steps 2 and 3, then the next 3 treble to the back, repeating steps 5 and 6 alternately across the row. Work last treble to front, going round turning chain at end of row.

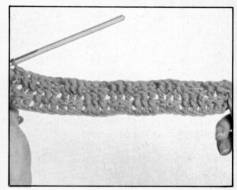

9 Turn and make 2 chain as before. The trebles which were at the front on the previous row now appear to be at the back and vice versa. Miss 1st (edge) stitch and work each of next 2 treble to front, repeating steps 2 and 3, so that they are now brought forward.

10 Now work each of next 3 treble to the back, repeating steps 5 and 6, so that they are taken to back of work. You will see that the fabric is reversible.

11 Continue to alternate the position of the blocks of trebles across the row, so that each forward block is taken back and vice versa. Work last treble round the turning chain in correct pattern sequence.

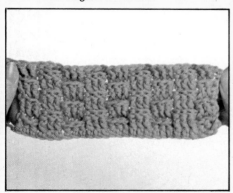

12 Work rows alternately in this way each time to create the woven effect. Several rows have been worked here, and you will see that where stitches have been worked to the back a ridge is formed running horizontally across fabric.

13 This sample shows blocks of 6 treble worked in same way, but with 2 rows worked before alternating position, so that the forward stitches will be kept back on the 2nd pattern row, before changing position on following row, to produce a strongly vertical pattern.

14 This sample shows the effect of working 1 treble to the front and then one to the back all the way across the row. The position of the trebles is reversed each time on every row to produce this woven, lattice effect.

Fred Mancini

Although they are worked in different ways, these three patterns all suggest basket work in their textures.

Elongated basket stitch

Here you must work into the row two rows below, placing the hook between the stitches each time to make the long trebles. The pattern is worked over a number of chain divisible by 6 plus 3, with 2 extra for the turning chain.

1st row 1tr into 4th ch from hook, 1 tr into each ch to end. Turn.
2nd row 1ch, miss first st, 1dc into each st to end. Turn.
3rd row (WS) 3ch, miss first st, 1tr into each of next 2 sts, *(yrh and insert hook between next 2 tr in row below, yrh and draw yarn up to same height as row being worked, complete treble in normal way – called 1tr below – 3 times, 1tr into each of next 3 sts working in to top of stitch in normal way – called 1tr top – rep from * to end, working last tr into turning chain. Turn.
4th row (RS) As 2nd.
5th row 3ch, 1 tr below between 1st and 2nd tr in row below, 1tr below between next 2 tr, *1tr top into each of next 3dc, (1tr below between next 2tr) 3 times, rep from * to end, working last tr below between last tr and turning chain. Turn.
6th row As 4th.
3rd to 6th rows form patt and are rep throughout.

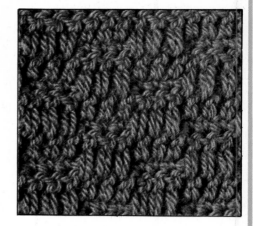

Basket weave variation

Unlike the basket weave stitches illustrated in the step-by-step photographs, this pattern has a definite right and wrong side to it. It is worked over a number of chain divisible by 10 plus 7, with 2 extra for the turning chain.

1st row (RS) 1tr into 4th ch from hook, 1tr into each ch to end. Turn.
2nd row 3ch, miss first tr, yrh and insert hook from right to left from back to front, round stem of next tr and to back of work again, yrh and draw through a loop, yrh and draw through 2 loops yrh and draw through rem 2 loops – 1 treble back; 1trB round each of next 4tr, *1tr into each of next 5tr in normal way, 1trB round each of next 5tr, rep from * to end, 1tr into top of turning chain. Turn.
3rd row 3ch, miss first tr, yrh, insert hook between 2nd and 3rd, from front to back, round stem of next tr and to the front again, yrh and draw through a loop, yrh and draw through 2 loops on hook, yrh and draw through rem 2 loops – 1 treble front, or 1tr F – round each of next 4tr, *1 tr into each of next 5tr in normal way, 1tr F round each of next 5tr, rep from * to end, 1tr into top of turning chain. Turn.
4th row As 2nd.
5th row 3ch, miss first tr, 1tr into each of next 5tr in normal way, *1trF round each of next 5tr, 1tr into each of next 5tr in normal way, rep from * to end, 1tr into top of turning chain. Turn.
6th row 3ch, miss first tr, 1tr into each of next 5tr in normal way, *1trB round each of next 5tr, 1tr into each of next 5tr in normal way, rep from * to end, 1tr into top of turning chain. Turn.
7th row As 5th.
8th row As 6th.
9th row As 3rd.
10th row As 2nd.
The 3rd to 10th rows form pattern. Rep them throughout until the fabric is the depth you require.

Raised treble pattern

Here trebles worked round the stem are worked alternately with trebles worked in the normal way to produce a highly textured, almost double fabric, similar in appearance to honeycomb stitch but made in squares rather than diamond shapes. The pattern is worked over an uneven number of stitches, and you should begin by making an uneven number of chain of any length.
1st row 1tr into 4th ch from hook, 1tr into each ch to end. Turn.
2nd row 3ch, miss first tr, *1tr round stem of next tr inserting hook from right to left from the front to the back and round to the front of the work again— 1 treble front – 1 tr into top of next st in normal way, rep from * to end, 1tr into top of turning chain. Turn.
3rd row 3ch, miss first tr, 1tr into top of next tr in normal way, 1trF round next tr, rep from * to last 2tr, 1tr into next tr, 1tr into top of turning chain. Turn.
4th row As 2nd row, but ending with 1trF, 1tr into top of turning chain. Turn.
5th row As 3rd.
4th and 5th rows form pattern and are repeated throughout. Note that you alternate the trebles on each row by working 1trF into the normal treble worked in previous row and vice versa each time. Continue in this way to the required depth.

Mat finish

This bath mat is just the thing for catching splashes and drips. It is worked in a thick cotton with a sturdy basket weave pattern and is trimmed round three sides with a short fringe.

Gary Warren

Size
42cm wide by 69cm long, excluding fringe.

Materials
8 x 50g balls of Twilleys Dishcloth 77 cotton for mat ; 2 balls for fringe
3.50mm crochet hook

Tension
1 patt rep (12sts) to 6cm and 16 rows to 13cm over patt on 3.50mm hook.

To make
Using 3.50mm hook make 140 ch.
Base row 1tr into 4th ch from hook. 1tr into each ch to end. Turn.
Commence patt.
1st row (RS) 2ch, work *round* each of next 5tr by working yrh, insert hook from front to back between next 2tr, round tr at left and through work from back to front ; draw yarn through and complete tr in usual way—called treble round front (tr round Ft), work *round* each of next 6tr by working yrh, insert hook from back to front between next 2tr, round tr at left and through work from front to to back ; draw yarn through and complete tr in usual way—called 1 treble round back (tr round Bk), now work *6tr round Ft, 6tr round Bk, rep from * to within last 6sts, tr round Front to end. Turn.
2nd row 2ch, work 5tr round Bk, 6tr round Ft, *6tr round Bk, 6tr round Ft, rep from * to within last 6sts, tr round Bk to end. Turn.
3rd row As 1st row.
4th row As 1st row.
5th row As 2nd row.

6th row As 1st row.
These 6 rows form the patt. Rep them 7 times more, then work 1st to 3rd rows again.
Fasten off.

Fringe
Using four strands of yarn together, knot fringe into every alternate row end along each short edge and into every alternate st along one long edge.
Trim the ends.

One for the boys

This bomber-style jacket has a thick textured basket weave pattern for extra warmth. Contrasting collar, cuffs and welt add a touch of style.

Sizes
To fit 66[71:76]cm chest.
Length, 42[46:50]cm.
Sleeve seam, 38[40:42]cm.
Note Instructions for larger sizes are in square brackets []; where there is only one set of figures it applies to all sizes.

Materials
12[13:14] x 50g balls of Sunbeam
Aran Knit in main colour (A)
2 balls in a contrasting colour (B)
4.50mm and 5.50mm crochet hooks
35[40:45]cm open-ended zip
fastener
10cm zip fastener for pocket

Tension
14 sts and 14 rows to 10cm over patt on 5.50mm hook.

Back
**Using 4.50mm hook and B, make 52 [56:60] ch.
Base row 1dc into 3rd ch from hook, 1dc into each ch to end. Turn.
Next row 2ch to count as first dc, 1dc into each dc to end. Turn.
Rep the last row 4 times more. Cut off B, join to A. Change to 5.50mm hook.
Work 2 rows in dc. Commence patt.
1st row (RS) 3ch to count as first tr, *1tr into next dc, work round next tr by working yrh, insert hook from front to back between next 2tr, round tr at left and through work from back to front; draw yarn through and complete tr in usual way—called treble round front (tr round Ft), rep from * to within last 2dc, 1tr into next dc, 1tr into turning ch. Turn.
2nd row 2ch, 1 dc into each st. Turn.
3rd row 3ch, *work 1tr round Ft working round next tr on first row, miss dc above this tr, 1tr into next dc, rep from * to end, working last tr into turning ch. Turn.
4th row As 2nd row.
5th row 3ch, 1tr into next dc, *1tr round front working round next tr on 3rd row, miss dc above this tr, 1tr into next dc, rep from * to within turning ch, 1tr into turning ch. Turn.
The 2nd to 5th rows form the patt. *
Cont in patt until work measures 28[30:32]cm from beg, ending with a WS row.
Shape armholes
Next row Ss over first 5sts, patt to within last 4sts, turn.

Serge Krouglikoff/kite from The Kite Shop

John Hutchinson

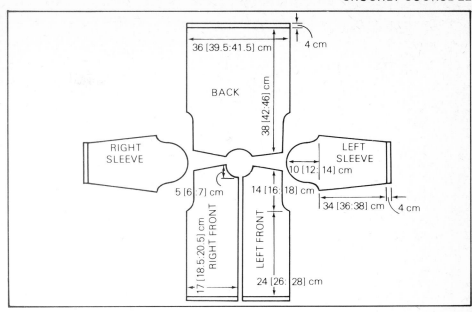

Dec one st at each end of next 2[3:4] rows by working 2dc tog. 39[41:43]dc. Cont without shaping until work measures 14[16:18]cm from beg of armhole shaping, ending with a WS row.

Shape shoulders

Next row Ss over first 5[5:6]sts, patt over next 5[6:6]sts. Fasten off. Miss next 19 sts, rejoin yarn to next st, patt over next 5[6:6] sts. Fasten off.

Left front

Using 4.50mm hook and B, make 26[28:30] ch.
Work as given for back from ** to **.
Cont in patt until work measures 14cm from beg, ending with a WS row.

Pocket row Patt over first 5[6:7] sts, make 15ch, miss next 15sts, patt over last 5[6:7] sts. Turn.
Cont in patt, working into ch on next row, until front measures same as back up to armhole, ending with a WS row.

Shape armhole

Next row Ss over first 5 sts, patt to end. Turn. 19[20:21] sts. Dec one st at armhole edge on next 2[3:4] rows. Cont without shaping until work measures 9[10:11]cm from beg of armhole shaping, ending with a WS row.

Shape neck

Next row Patt to within last 4 sts, turn. Dec one st at neck edge on next 5 rows, then cont without shaping until armhole measures the same as back, up to beg of shoulder shaping, ending with a WS row.

Shape shoulder

Next row Ss over first 5[5:6] sts, patt to end. Fasten off.

Right front

Work to match left front, omitting pocket and reversing all shaping.

Sleeves

Using 4.50mm hook and B, make 22[24:26] ch. Work base row as given for back, then work 5 rows in dc, inc

4[4:6]dc evenly on last row by working 2dc into a dc. 25[27:31]dc.
Cut off B, join on A. Change to 5.50mm hook and work 2 rows dc.
Cont in patt as given for back but in one st at each end of 3rd and every foll 8th row until there are 35[39:43] sts. Cont wthout shaping until sleeve measures 38[40:42]cm from beg, ending with a WS row.

Shape top

Next row Ss over first 5 sts, patt to within last 4 sts. Turn. Work 1 row. Dec one st at each end of next and foll 3[4:5] alt rows, then at each end of every row until 9 sts rem. Fasten off.

Collar

Using 4.50mm hook and B, make 57[61:65] ch loosely.
Work base row as given for back, then work 3 rows in dc.
Next row 2ch, 1dc into each of next 5[4:5]dc, * work next 2dc tog, 1dc into each of next 12[10-8]dc, rep from * 2[3:4] times more, work next 2dc tog, 1dc into each dc to end. Turn. 52[55:58] dc. Work 3 rows.
Next row 2ch, 1dc into each of next 5[4:5]dc, *work next 2dc tog, 1dc into each of next 11[9:7]dc, rep from * 2[3:4] times more, work next 2dc tog, 1dc into each dc to end. Turn. 48[50:52]dc. Work 1[3:5] rows.
Next row Ss over first 5sts, patt to within last 4sts. Turn.
Rep last row 3 times more. Fasten off.

To make up

Join shoulder seams. Set in sleeves, then join side and sleeve seams. Sew zip into pocket opening. Make pocket lining and sew in position.
Join on yarn and, using 4.50mm hook, work 2 rows of dc evenly along each front edge, matching colours. Sew in zip. Sew on collar. Press seams.

Step-by-step course – 23

*Vertical chains worked on a crochet background
*Making the background fabric
*Working the vertical chains
*Pattern for a man's slipover

Vertical chains worked on a crochet background

In this course we show you how to work crochet chains vertically on to a basic background fabric to make striped, checked and plaid patterns. These patterns are fun to work; you'll enjoy creating your own designs and using oddments of yarn in imaginative ways. Remember, though, that before you start you must work out the sequence in which the colours are to be used, since you could otherwise end up with a haphazard and untidy-looking fabric.

You can either work the background in a plain colour, using one or more contrasting colours for the vertical chains, or work it in a horizontal stripe pattern – again using contrasting colours for the chains – to create a more intricate pattern.

The fabric is worked in two stages. The first stage is to make a background, leaving spaces into which the chains can be worked. This can be an all-over lattice pattern, in which case you will need to work the lines of chain evenly across the width of the fabric, filling in all the spaces. Or it can consist of blocks of treble interspersed with lattice pattern so that the crochet chains will only be worked at intervals across the fabric. The second stage is, of course, to work the lines of chain vertically up and down or across the fabric.

Making the background fabric

For the sample in steps 1-6 use a double knitting yarn and 4.00mm hook.

1 Begin by making an uneven number of chain. Work 1 treble into the 5th chain from the hook. (These 5 chain count as first treble, missed chain and 1 chain). Make 1 chain. Miss next chain and work 1 treble into next chain.

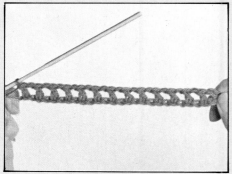

2 Now work 1 chain, miss next chain and work 1 treble into next chain all the way across the row, working last treble into last chain.

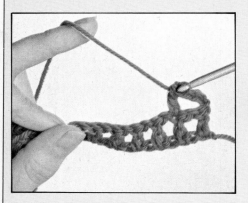

3 Turn and work 4 chain (to count as first treble and 1 chain). Miss first (edge) treble and space and work 1 treble into next treble.

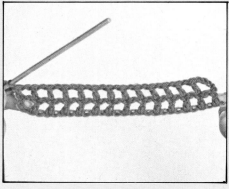

4 Continue to work 1 chain, miss 1 space and 1 treble into next treble all the way across the row. Work the last treble into the 4th of first 5 chain to complete the row.

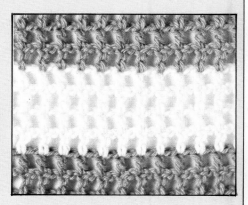

5 Continue to repeat steps 3 and 4, working last tr into 3rd of 4 chain, for each row of the lattice pattern. We used 2 colours for our sample, working 4 rows in each colour throughout. Fasten off.

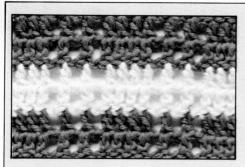

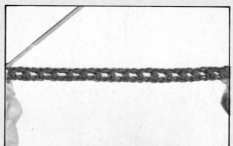

6 This sample shows a background fabric in which blocks of solid trebles and lattice stripes have been worked alternately across the row. In this case 4 treble have been alternated with 3 lattice spaces and worked in a striped pattern using two colours.

7 When using a 4-ply yarn it may be necessary to use half trebles in order to make the stitches the right proportion. A 4-ply yarn worked in trebles will tend to produce a rather loose fabric. Half trebles will make a firmer fabric and will leave shorter spaces which can be more easily filled with chain. In this case, work the background as before, substituting half trebles for trebles throughout. You will have to begin with an uneven number of chain and work the first half treble into fifth chain from hook.

8 On subsequent rows, work 3 chain to count as the first half treble and 1 chain at the beginning of the row, instead of the 4 chain worked when using trebles for the background.

Working the vertical chains

The chain stitch used is essentially the same as that used in embroidery, even though it is worked with a crochet hook. Normally a double thickness of yarn is used for the chains.

You can either use two balls of yarn at the same time, or – provided that the piece to be covered is not very long – cut a length approximately eight times the required length of the finished chain and fold it in half. (In this case you may not need to begin by making a slip loop, as in our sample, but can simply place the doubled yarn over the hook.)

1 Keep the RS of the background fabric facing you as you work. Make a slip loop on the hook, then insert the hook from front to back into the bottom right-hand corner space.

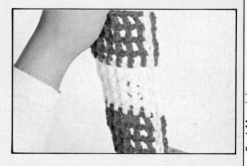

2 Wind the double yarn round the hook and draw it through the space and then through the loop on the hook. Always keep the ball of yarn at the back of the work.

3 Draw the loop up slightly and insert the hook from front to back into the next space. It is important to keep the yarn fairly slack when working each chain in order to avoid distorting the background fabric.

4 Repeat step 2 to complete this chain. Continue to work chains in this way all the way up the fabric, working into each space. Make the last chain over the top edge of the fabric and pull yarn through to fasten off.

Fred Mancini

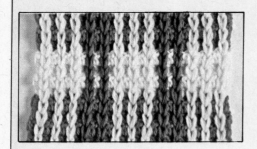

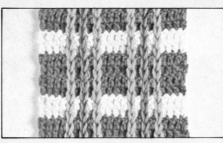

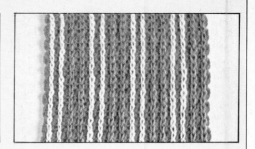

5 This sample shows each vertical line worked in chains, using one of the background colours and a contrast colour to create a simple check pattern. You will have to sew the spare ends of yarn to the WS of fabric when it is completed.

6 Here the background fabric previously worked, which combines blocks of trebles and lattice pattern, has been completed by working the vertical chain lines in two contrast colours to achieve a plaid effect.

7 A single thickness of 4-ply yarn has been used to make the chains on this sample, in which half trebles were used instead of trebles to create the background fabric. You will often find that you need to experiment with different-sized hooks and different background fabrics to obtain the desired effect in your chosen yarn. In some cases a single thickness of yarn works better than a double thickness.

Check mate

Your man won't mind being in check when he wears this smart slipover. Worked in half trebles, the fabric has contrasting checks, with the vertical lines worked in chain.

Sizes
To fit 97[102:107:112]cm chest.
Length, 61[62:63:64]cm.

Note Instructions for larger sizes are in square brackets []; where there is only one set of figures it applies to all sizes.

Materials
13[13:13:14] x 25g balls of Wendy Nylonised 4 ply in main colour (A)
2 balls in each of 2 contrasting colours (B) and (C)
3.00mm and 3.50mm crochet hooks

Tension
20 sts and 16 rows to 10cm over patt using 3.50mm hook.

Back
**Using 3.50mm hook and A, make 103[109:115:120]ch.
Base row 1htr into 3rd ch from hook, 1htr into each ch to end. Turn.
102[108:114:119] sts.
1st row (WS) 2ch to count as first htr, 1htr into each of next 10[13:13:16] htr,
*1ch, miss next htr, 1htr into each of next 3htr, 1ch, miss next htr, 1htr into each of next 20[20:22:22]htr, rep from * twice

Victor Yuan/accessories from Howie

more, 1ch, miss next htr, 1htr into each of next 3htr, 1ch, miss next htr, 1htr into each of last 11[14 :14 :17]htr. Turn.
2nd row 2ch, 1htr into each of next 10[13 :13 :16]htr, *1ch, 1htr into each of next 3htr, 1ch, 1htr into each of next 20[20 :22 :22]htr, rep from * twice more, 1ch, 1htr into each of next 3htr, 1ch, 1htr into each of last 11[14 :14 :17]htr. Turn.
3rd - 5th rows As 2nd row, but joining on B on last htr of 5th row.
6th row Using B, work as 2nd row, cut off B, do not turn, but return to beg of row, so working in the same direction as last row.
7th row RS facing and using A, work as 2nd row. Turn.
8th row As 2nd row, but joining on C on last htr. Turn.
9th row Using C, work as 2nd row, cut off C, do not turn but return to beg of row.
10th row RS facing and using A, work as 2nd row. Turn.
11th – 25th rows As 2nd row, but joining on B on last htr of 25th row.
The 6th to 25th rows form the patt. Cont in patt until work measures 37cm from beg. **

Shape armholes
Next row SS over first 5htr, 2ch, patt to within last 4htr, turn.
Next row Ss over first 3htr, 2ch, patt to within last 2htr, turn.
Work 2htr tog (to dec one htr) at each end of next 2[3 :3 :4] rows, then at each end of foll 2[2 :3 :3] alt rows. 82[86 :90 :94]htr. Cont without shaping until work measures 24[25 :26 :27]cm from beg of armhole shaping.
Shape shoulder
Next row Ss over first 7[8 :8 :8]htr, 2ch, patt to within last 6[7 :7 :7]htr, turn.
Rep this row twice more.
Next row Ss over first 6[5 :5 :7]htr, 2ch, patt to within last 5[4 :4 :6]htr. Fasten off.

Front
Work as given for back from ** to **.
Shape armhole and divide for neck
Next row Ss over first 5htr, 2ch, patt 46[49 :52 :55]htr, turn.
Work on this set of sts first.
Next row Dec 1htr, patt to within last 2htr, turn.
Dec 1htr at armhole edge on next and foll 1[2 :2 :3] rows, then on foll 2[2 :3 :3] alt rows *and at the same time* dec one htr at neck edge on every foll alt row until 23[25 :25 :27]htr rem. Cont without shaping until work measures 24[25 :26 :27]cm from beg of armhole shaping, ending with a WS row.

Shape shoulder
Next row Ss over first 7[8 :8 :8]htr, 2ch, patt to end. Turn.
Next row Patt to last 6[7 :7 :7]htr. Turn.
Next row Ss over first 7[8 :8 :8]htr, 2ch, patt to end. Turn.
Next row Patt to within last 5[4 :4 :6]htr. Fasten off. Rejoin yarn to rem sts at centre front neck and complete to match first side reversing all shapings.

To work vertical chains
Work chain stitch up the spaces in patt make a slip loop on hook as foll. Using B and keeping yarn at back of work insert the hook into the first sp and draw a loop through, *insert hook into next sp, yrh and draw a loop through the loop on the hook, rep from * working fairly loosely all the way up the garment. Fasten off. Cont to work into all the chain spaces across the row alternating B and C.

To make up
Press work with a warm iron over a damp cloth. Join shoulder and side seams.
Neck: Using 3.00 hook and A, work 4 rows of dc evenly all round neck edge working (2dc together) twice at centre front on every row. **Armholes:** Using 3.00mm hook and A, work 4 rows of dc evenly all round armhole. **Welt:** Using 3.00mm hook and A, work 8 rows of dc evenly all round lower edge.

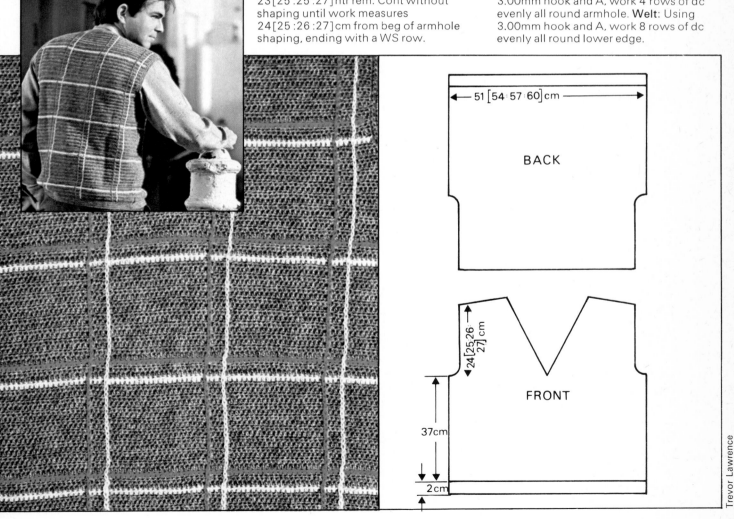

Step-by-step course – 24

Working shell patterns

Shell patterns are among the most popular crochet stitches, and fortunately, there is an amazing variety of them from which to choose. One advantage of shell patterns is that they look good whether worked in a fine cotton or in a thicker knitting yarn.

The basic principle of shell patterns – working three or more stitches into one stitch – can be used in many ways. If the stitches are all the same kind, the shell produced will be a simple fan shape. Alternatively, by working a series of different stitches which gradually increase and then decrease in height – for example, from a double crochet through to a double treble and back again to a double crochet – you can make a dome-shaped shell. For an open effect you can work one chain between each stitch. Whatever type of stitches are used, the pattern will normally call for an uneven number of them to be worked in each shell.

Here we give you step-by-step instructions for two different patterns. Once you have practised them you will find the shell stitch featured in the long-line waistcoat simple to work.

Simple shell pattern

This pattern is a perfect example of trebles and double crochet used alternatively on each row to produce an all-over shell pattern. It is worked over a multiple of 6 chain with 2 extra for the turning chain. Our sample uses a double knitting yarn and a 4.50mm hook and is worked on a foundation of 26 chain.

1 Make the first shell by working 3 treble, 1 chain and 3 treble all into the 5th chain from the hook. The first 4 chain will count as the first double crochet and 2 chain.

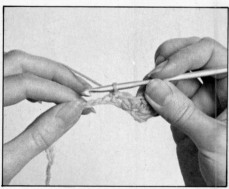

2 Miss the next 2 chain and work 1 double crochet into the following chain.

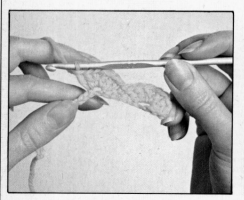

3 Miss the next 2 chain. Now work another shell in the same way as before into the next chain.

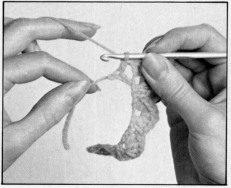

4 Continue to repeat steps 2 and 3 all the way along the chain until only 3 chain remain unworked. Miss the next 2 chain and work 1 treble into the last chain.

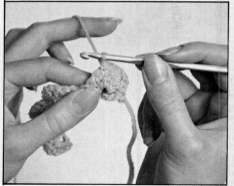

5 Turn and work 3 chain as the first treble. Now work 1 double crochet into the centre chain between the trebles in the first shell.

Fred Mancini

continued : Simple shell pattern

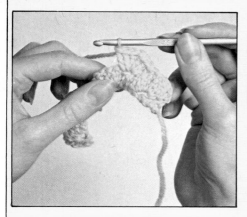

6 Now work 1 shell in the same way as before into the double crochet between the first and 2nd shells.

7 Continue to work 1 double crochet into the middle of each shell and 1 shell into each double crochet between the shells in the previous row until 1 shell remains unworked.

8 Now work 1 double crochet into the centre of the last shell.

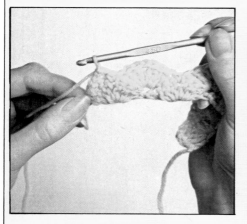

9 Work 1 treble into the turning chain of the previous row to complete the 2nd row.

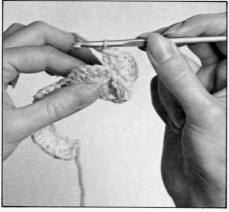

10 Turn and work 2 chain to count as the first double crochet. Now work 1 shell into the first double crochet of the previous row.

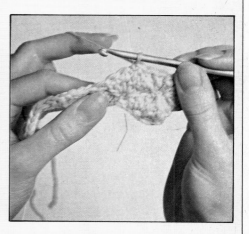

11 Now work 1 double crochet into the centre of the next shell.

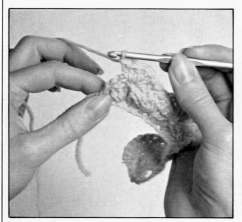

12 Continue to work across the row as before, working 1 shell into each double crochet and 1 double crochet into each shell until only the turning chain remains unworked in the previous row.

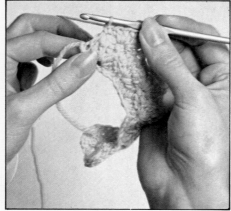

13 Now work 1 double crochet into the turning chain to complete 3rd row.

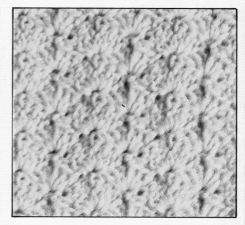

14 Continue to alternate the shell on each row in the same way, beginning each subsequent row with either 2 chain for a double crochet or 3 chain for a treble to keep the pattern correct.

Open shell pattern

This very simple pattern produces a pretty, open effect which is particularly effective when worked in crochet cotton. Our sample is based on 31 chain and worked in a 4-ply yarn with a 4.00mm hook. If you wish to make the sample larger or smaller, use any multiple of 4 chain plus 3 extra for the turning chain.

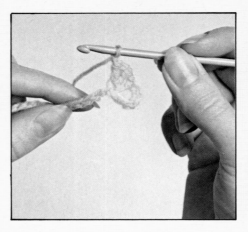

1 Make the first shell by working (1 treble and 1 chain) 3 times, all into the 7th chain from the hook.

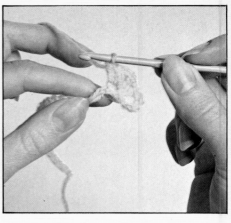

2 Now work 1 more treble into the same chain so that there are 4 trebles with 1 chain between each in the completed shell.

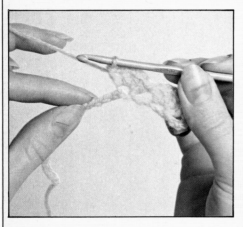

3 Miss the next 3 chain and work another shell in exactly the same way into the next chain. The centre of the shell is the 2nd 1-chain space.

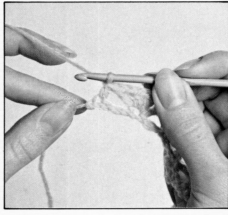

4 Repeat step 3 all along the chain until 4 chain remain unworked. Miss the next 3 chain and work 1 treble into the last chain to complete the first row.

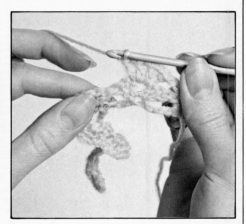

5 Turn and work 3 chain to count as the first treble. Work 1 shell in the same way as before into the centre 1-chain space of the first shell in the previous row.

6 Work 1 shell into the centre of each shell in the same way all along the row until the last shell only remains unworked.

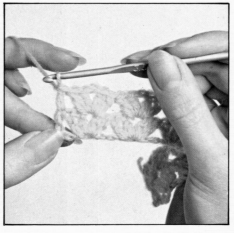

7 Work 1 shell into the last shell. Now work 1 treble into the turning chain to complete the 2nd row.

8 Continue to work each row in the same way, repeating steps 5-7 each time.

Stitch Wise

Shell Trellis Pattern

This classic pattern, in which the shells are worked in vertical lines with chain bars between each, has many variations. Our version combines trebles, double crochet and chain spaces to make a very pretty pattern, which looks equally good worked in a fine or thick yarn. Now that you have learnt the basic method for working shell patterns, try making a sample of this stitch for future reference. Make 32 chain.

Base row 1dc into 8th ch from hook, *3ch, miss next 2ch, 1dc into next ch, 2ch, miss next 2ch, 1tr into next ch, 2ch, miss next 2ch, 1dc into next ch, rep from * to last 6 ch, 3ch, miss next 2ch, 1dc into next ch, 2ch, miss next 2ch, 1 treble into last ch. Turn. 9h sp.

1st row 2ch, miss first 2ch sp, * work (2tr, 1ch, 2tr, 1ch, 2tr) all into next 3ch sp – called 1 shell – ; 1ch, 1dc into next tr in previous row, 1ch, rep from * to last 3ch sp, 1 shell into this sp, miss next 2ch, 1dc into next chain. Turn.

2nd row 5ch, * work 1dc into space between first 2 pairs of trebles in first shell, 3ch, 1dc into space between next 2 pairs of trebles in same shell, 2ch, 1tr into next dc in previous row, 2ch, rep from * to last shell, 1dc into space between first 2 pairs of trebles in last shell, 3ch, 1dc into space between next 2 pairs of trebles in same shell, 2ch, 1tr into turning chain. Turn.

These last 2 rows form patt and are repeated throughout.

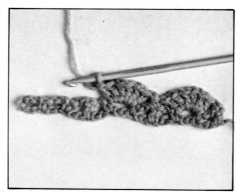

A shell worked into the 3 chain space made in the base row.

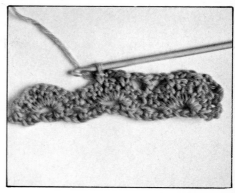

A double crochet worked into either side of the shell to form the base for the shell in the next row.

Several rows of the completed pattern.

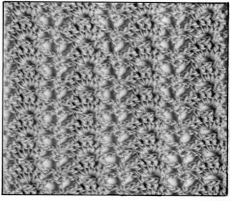

The versatility of crochet – the same stitch worked in a fine crochet cotton.

Long and lacy

The perennially popular waistcoat can be worn in many ways. Our version — worked in a shell stitch using a mohair type yarn — is shown here belted and bloused, but it looks just as good worn loose.

Sizes
To fit 87[92:97]cm bust.
Length, 81cm.
Note Instructions for larger sizes are in square brackets []. Where there is only one set of figures it applies to all sizes.

Materials
11[12:12] x 50g balls of Jaeger Gabrielle
5.50mm crochet hook

Tension
1 patt repeat measures 6cm in width and 2 patt repeats measure 6cm in depth worked on a 5.50mm hook.

Left front
** Using 5.50mm hook make 33[35:38] ch.
Base row 1dc into 3rd ch from hook, 1dc into each ch to end. Turn. 32[34:37] dc.
Next row 2ch to count as first dc, 1dc into each dc to end, working last dc into the turning ch. Turn.
Rep last row 3 times more. **
Commence patt.
The patt rows for each size are given separately. Follow the appropriate instructions for the size that you are making.

1st size only
1st row (RS) 3ch to count as first tr, * miss next 3dc, 7tr all into next dc – shell formed, miss next 3dc, 1tr into each of next 2dc, rep from * twice more, miss next 3dc, 4tr into last dc – half shell formed. Turn.
2nd row 5ch to count as first dc and 3ch, *1tr into each of next 2 single tr, 3ch, 1dc into centre tr of next shell, 3ch, rep from * twice more, 1tr into last tr. Turn.
3rd row 3ch, *1 shell into next dc at centre of previous shell, 1tr into each of next 2tr, rep from * twice more, 4tr into 2nd of the 5ch. Turn.
The 2nd and 3rd rows form patt for the 1st size.

2nd size only
1st row (RS) 3ch to count as first tr, 1tr into each of next 2dc, *miss next 3dc, 7tr all into next dc – shell formed, miss next 3dc, 1tr into each of next 2dc, rep from * twice more, miss next 3dc, 4tr into last dc – half shell formed. Turn.

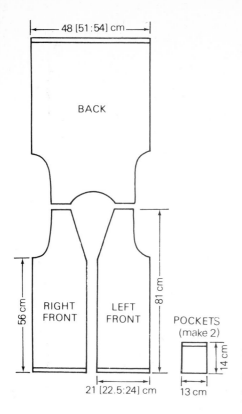

48 [51:54] cm

BACK

RIGHT FRONT

LEFT FRONT

POCKETS (make 2)

56 cm

81 cm

14 cm

21 [22.5:24] cm

13 cm

John Hutchinson

2nd row 5ch to count as first dc and 3ch, *1tr into each of next 2 single tr, 3ch, 1dc into centre tr of next shell, 3ch, rep from * twice more, 1tr into each of last 3tr. Turn.

3rd row 3ch, 1tr into each of next 2tr, *1 shell into dc at centre of previous shell, 1tr into each of next 2tr, rep from * twice more, 4tr into 2nd of the 5ch. Turn. The 2nd and 3rd rows form patt for the 2nd size.

3rd size only
1st row (RS) 3ch to count as first tr, 3tr into first dc, miss next 3dc, 1tr into each of next 2dc, *miss next 3dc, 7tr all into next dc – shell formed, miss next 3dc, 1tr into each of next 2dc, rep from * twice more, miss next 3dc, 4tr into last dc – half shell formed. Turn.

2nd row 5ch to count as first dc and 3ch, *1tr into each of next 2 single tr, 3ch, 1dc into centre tr of next shell, 3ch, rep from * twice more, 1tr into each of next 2 single tr, 3ch, 1dc into last tr. Turn.

3rd row 3ch, 3tr into first dc, *1tr into each of next 2tr, 1 shell into dc at centre of previous shell, rep from * twice more, 1tr into each of next 2tr, 4tr into 2nd of the 5ch. Turn. The 2nd and 3rd rows form patt for the 3rd size.

All sizes
Cont in patt until work measures 56cm from beg, ending with a 3rd patt row.

Shape armhole
Next row Patt to last 9sts (including turning ch), turn and leave these sts unworked.

Shape neck
1st row Patt to within last 4ch, work 2tr into ch, now work 2tr tog.
2nd row 2ch to count as first st, 1tr into each of next 2tr, work in patt to end of row. Turn.
3rd row Patt to within last 2sts, work 2tr tog. Turn.
Cont to dec one st at neck edge on every alt row in the same way until 16[18:21] sts rem.
Next row 4ch, 1dc into centre tr of next shell, patt to end. Turn.
Next row Patt to within last dc, 4tr into last dc, 1tr into each of next 2ch. Turn. 16sts.
Rep these 2 rows until armhole measures 25cm from beg. Fasten off.

Right front
Work as given for left front from ** to **. Commence patt.
1st size only
1st row (RS) 3ch to count as first tr, 3tr into first st, miss next 3dc, *1tr into each of next 2dc, miss next 3dc, 1 shell into next dc, miss next 3dc, rep from * twice more, 1 tr into last tr. Turn.
This sets patt for the 1st size.
2nd size only
1st row (RS) 3ch to count as first tr, 3tr into first st, miss next 3dc, *1tr into each of next 2dc, miss next 3dc, 1 shell into next dc, rep from * twice more, 1 tr into each of last 3dc. Turn.
This sets patt for 2nd size.
3rd size only
1st row (RS) 3ch to count as first tr, 3tr into first st, miss next 3dc, *1 tr into each of next 2dc, miss next 3dc, 1 shell into next dc, rep from * twice more, 1tr into each of next 3dc, miss next 3dc, 4tr into last dc. Turn.
This sets patt for 3rd size.
All sizes
Cont in patt as set until work measures same as left front to armhole, ending with a 3rd patt row. Fasten off and turn work.
Shape armhole
Next row Miss first 9sts. Rejoin yarn to next st, 2ch, patt to end. Turn.
Complete as given for left front, reversing neck shaping.

Back
Using 5.50mm hook make 73[77:83] ch. Work base row as given for left front. 72[76:82] sts. Work 4 rows in dc. Commence patt.
1st size only
1st row (RS) 3ch to count as first tr, *miss next 3dc, 1 shell into next dc, miss next 3dc, 1tr into each of next 2 dc, rep from * to within last 8dc, miss next 3dc, 1 shell into next dc, miss next 3dc, 1tr into last dc. Turn.
This sets patt for the 1st size.
2nd size only
1st row (RS) 3ch to count as first tr,

1tr into each of next 2dc, *miss next 3dc, 1 shell into next dc, miss next 3 dc, 1tr into each of next 2dc, rep from * to within last dc, 1tr into last dc. Turn.
This sets patt for the 2nd size.
3rd size only
1st row (RS) 3ch to count as first tr, 3tr into first dc, miss next 3dc, 1tr into each of next 2dc, *miss next 3dc, 1 shell into next dc, miss next 3dc, 1tr into each of next 2dc, rep from * to within last 4dc, miss next 3dc, 4tr into last dc. Turn.
This sets patt for the 3rd size.
All sizes
Cont in patt as set until work measures same as left front to armholes, ending with a 3rd patt row. Fasten off and turn work.
Shape armholes
Next row Miss first 9sts, rejoin yarn to next st, work 2ch, patt to within last 9sts, turn and leave these 9sts unworked.
Cont in patt until armholes measure same as left front, ending with a 3rd patt row. Fasten off.

Pockets (make 2)
Using 5.50mm hook make 21ch.
Base row 4tr into 3rd ch from hook, miss next 3ch, 1tr into each of next 2ch, miss next 3ch, 1shell into next ch, miss next 3ch, 1tr into each of next 2ch, miss next 3ch, 4tr into last ch. Turn.
Work 6 rows in patt as set.
Next row Work 1dc into each st to end, decr 4sts evenly across the row. Turn.
Work 4 more rows in dc. Fasten off.

To make up
Do not press. Join shoulder seams.
Front border
With RS of right front facing and beg at lower edge, work a row of dc ip right front to shoulder, working 1dc into each row end of border and 2dc into each patt row end. Work 1dc into each st across back of neck and now work in dc down left front as before. Turn and work 4 rows in dc. Fasten off.
Armhole borders (alike)
Beg at side edge and work a row of dc round armhole edge, working 1dc into each st at underarm and 2dc into each patt row end.
1st row 1ch, now work 1dc into each of next 3sts, (work next 2dc tog) 3 times, now work 1dc into each dc until 10sts rem, (work 2dc tog) 3 times, 1dc into each of next 3sts, 1dc into turning ch. Turn.
2nd row 1ch, 1dc into each st to end. Turn
3rd row 1ch, 1dc into each of next 3sts, (work 2dc tog) 4 times, 1dc into each st until 11sts rem unworked, (work 2dc tog) 4 times, 1dc into each of next 2sts, 1dc into turning ch. Turn.
4th row As 2nd row. Fasten off.
Join side seams. Sew pockets to fronts.

Step-by-step course – 25

Working large lace patterns

There are several ways of making lace — on a loom or with bobbins, for example — but crocheted lace is probably the easiest method, since all you need is a crochet hook, some yarn and the ability to work all the basic crochet stitches that you have learned so far. The variety of patterns available is enormous, but basically they are all made in the same way : by building up groups of crochet stitches to form different shapes or motifs, such as shells or pyramids, and joining these with chain bars or single stitches. Don't be put off by the fact that some of these patterns appear complicated. They are much easier than they look, and as long as you follow the instructions carefully you will succeed in making a beautiful fabric. The type of lace fabric you make will, of course, depend on the thickness of yarn and the size of hook you use, but you will find that most of the patterns look equally good in a fine or a thick yarn.

Scallop shells

By working a simple pattern like the one shown here, you will begin to understand how large lace patterns are created. The basic principle is very similar however intricate the stitch might be, and thus, practising something quite simple like this scallop shell pattern will enable you to progress to a more complicated pattern without difficulty. To work this sample, first make 31 chain.

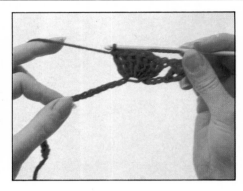

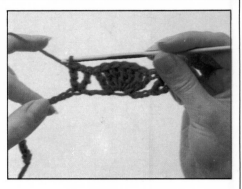

1 Work 1 double treble into 6th chain from hook. Miss next 3 chain and work 7 double treble into next chain for first shell. The chain are left unworked at each side of the shell or motif to create a space so that the motif can fan outwards and the fabric lies flat.

2 Miss next 3 chain. Now work 1 double treble, 1 chain and 1 double treble all into next chain. This 'V' group acts as a link between the shells. Lengths of chain and single stitches can also be used for this purpose, but you must still leave a space at either side of the group.

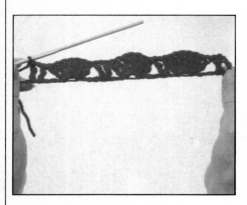

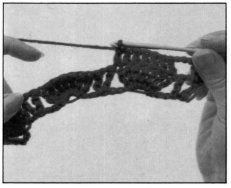

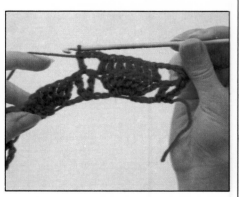

3 Work a shell and a V group alternately across the row in the same way. Make the last V group by working 1 double treble into the 2nd to last chain, 1 chain and the final double treble into the last chain. Most patterns will tell you exactly how to work the beginning and end of each row to maintain the continuity of the pattern.

4 Begin next row with 3 chain. Now work 1 treble into the first chain space. Work 3 chain and work 1 treble into each stitch in the first shell. Thus you begin to build up and enlarge the original shape. One chain is sometimes worked between these trebles to fan the motif outwards even further.

5 Make another 3 chain. Now work 1 treble into the centre of the next V group. The 3 chain and treble now form the link between the motifs in place of the V group, at the same time maintaining the open effect.

Paul Williams

118

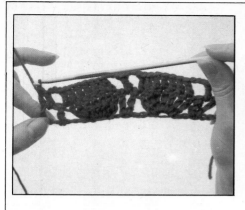

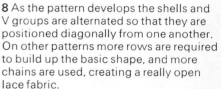

6 Continue to work into each shell and V group across the row, working 3 chain at each side. Finish the row with 1 treble into last space and 1 treble into turning chain. The last treble acts as the edge stitch.

7 The next row is worked in the same way as the first, except that the motifs are reversed by working a shell into each of the single trebles between the shells, and a V group into the centre stitch of each shell. To keep the pattern correct work 3 double treble at the beginning and end of the row to act as a half shell, since the full shell would be too wide.

8 As the pattern develops the shells and V groups are alternated so that they are positioned diagonally from one another. On other patterns more rows are required to build up the basic shape, and more chains are used, creating a really open lace fabric.

Japanese fan stitch

The soft fan shape of the shells in this pattern is achieved by working longer trebles than normal into one stitch. The resulting shell is much softer and thicker than it would normally be, creating a pretty, warm pattern, ideal for a cosy shawl.

The pattern is worked over a multiple of 14 chain plus 1. To make our sample work 30 chain (1 extra for the turning chain). Work 1 double crochet into 3rd chain and then 1 double crochet into each chain to end, so that there are 29 stitches in all. To make the sample wider, add 14 extra chain for each pattern repeat.

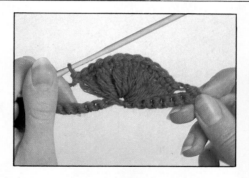

1 Turn and make 2 chain to count as first stitch. Miss next 6 stitches (7 including edge stitch). Now work 13 trebles into next stitch, drawing yarn out to about 1.25cm each time you work a treble, to make a long stitch. These 13 treble form first shell.

2 Miss next 6 stitches and work a double crochet into next stitch. Now miss next 6 stitches and work another shell into next stitch in same way as before. Miss next 6 stitches and work a double crochet into top of turning chain to complete first row.

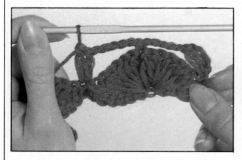

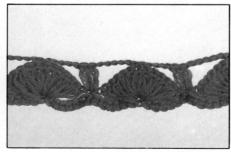

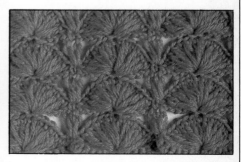

3 Now turn and work **4** chain. Work a long treble as before into first (edge) stitch. Now make 5 chain and work a double crochet into 7th (centre) trèble of next shell. Make 5 chain and work 2 long trebles into next double crochet between the shells.

4 Repeat these actions to complete the 2nd row, working 5 chain then a double crochet into the centre of the next shell ; 5 chain and then 2 long trebles into top of the turning chain.

5 To continue pattern turn and make 2 chain. Now work a shell as before into double crochet worked in centre of each shell in previous row and a double crochet between trebles worked in previous row, working last double crochet into top of turning chain. Continue to alternate 2nd and 3rd rows.

Paul Williams

Two lace patterns

Try working one or both of these two lace stitches. The first, shell and chain pattern, uses the more conventional method of working shell shapes and interlocking chains to produce an open-work lace fabric which could be worked in a fine cotton or thicker crochet yarn.

By contrast, the second pattern, Window Panes, makes use of square blocks of trebles and chain bars to create an unusual lace effect, which would be ideal for a bedspread, worked in a fairly thick cotton.

Window panes

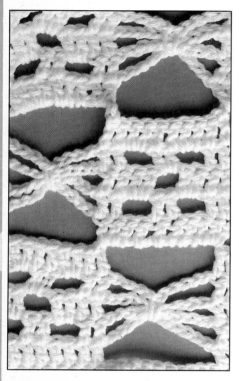

This pattern is worked over a multiple of 10 chain with 1 extra turning chain. We give instructions for working 3 blocks of pattern across the row. When using the pattern for a crochet fabric you will need to work extra stitches at either side to form a firm edge.

Make 31 chain ; work 29 double crochet into chain so having 30 stitches.

Base row 3ch, miss first st, 1tr into each of next 9dc, 10ch, miss 10dc, 1tr into each dc to end, working last tr into turning chain. Turn.

1st row 3ch, miss first st, 1tr into next st, *2ch, miss 2 sts, 1tr into each of next 2 sts, *, rep from * to * once more, 10ch, 1tr into each of next 2 sts, rep from * to * twice more, working last tr into turning chain. Turn.

2nd row 3ch, miss first st, 1tr into next st, * 2tr into next 2ch sp, 2ch, miss next 2 sts, 2tr into next 2ch sp, 1tr into each of next 2 sts*, 10ch, 1tr into each of next 2tr, rep from * to * once more, working last tr into turning chain. Turn.

3rd row 3ch, miss first st, 1tr into next st, * 2ch, miss 2 sts, 2tr into next 2ch sp, 2ch, miss 2 sts, 1tr into each of next 2tr *, 4ch, insert hook under first 10 chain loop from front to back, work 1dc round all 3 loops at centre to draw them together – called 1dc round ch ; 4ch, 1tr into each of next 2tr, rep from * to * once more, working last tr into turning chain. Turn.

4th row 3ch, miss first st, *1tr into each tr and 2tr into each 2ch sp*, 10ch, rep from * to * once more, working last tr into turning chain. Turn.

5th row 3ch to count as first tr, 10ch, 10tr into next 10ch loop, 10ch, 1tr into turning chain. Turn.

6th row 3ch to count as first tr, 10ch, 1tr into each of next 2tr, *2ch, miss 2 sts, 1tr into each of next 2 sts, rep from * once more, 10ch, 1tr into 3rd of first 3ch. Turn.

7th row 3ch to count as first tr, 10ch, 1tr into each of next 2tr, 2tr into 2ch sp, 2ch, miss 2 sts, 2tr into 2ch sp, 1tr into each of next 2tr, 10ch, 1tr into 3rd of first 3ch. Turn.

8th row 3ch to count as first tr, * 4ch, 1dc round ch, 4ch*, 1tr into each of next 2tr, 2ch, miss 2 sts, 2tr into next 2ch sp, 2ch, miss 2 sts, 1tr into each of next 2 sts, rep from * to * once more, 1 tr into 3rd of first 3ch. Turn.

9th row 3ch to count as first tr, 10ch, 1tr into each tr and 2tr into each 2ch sp, 10ch, 1tr into 3rd of 1st 3ch. Turn.

10th row 3ch, 9tr into 10ch loop, 10ch, 9tr into 10ch loop, 1 tr into 3rd of first 3ch. Turn. (10tr in each lattice section as before.)

Rows 1 to 10 form patt and are rep throughout so that position of squares is reversed each time. To work more squares across, repeat the lattice and chain sections alternately as many times as required, only working the turning chain at side edge.

Shell and chain pattern

This pattern is worked over a number of chain divisible by 10, plus 1 chain and 5 extra turning chain.

Base row (RS) 1tr into 6th ch from hook, *3ch, miss 3ch, 1dc into each of next 3ch, 3ch, miss 3ch, (1tr, 3ch, 1tr) all into next ch, rep from * ending last rep (1tr, 2ch, 1tr) all worked into last ch. Turn.

1st row 3ch, miss first tr, 3tr into first 2ch sp, *3ch, 1dc into 2nd of next 3dc, 3ch, 7tr into next 3ch sp between tr, rep from * to end, ending by working 3tr (half shell) instead of 7tr into last sp between tr and turning chain and last tr into top of turning ch. Turn.

2nd row 1ch, miss first st, 1dc into each of next 3tr, *5ch, 1dc into each of next 7tr, rep from * to last half shell, 5ch, 1dc into each of next 3tr, 1dc into 3rd of first 3ch. Turn.

3rd row 1ch, miss first dc, 1dc into next dc, *3ch, (1tr, 3ch, 1tr) all into 3rd of next 5ch, 3ch, miss first 2dc of next shell, 1dc into each of next 3dc, rep from * ending last rep, miss next 2dc, 1dc into

next dc, 1dc into first ch. Turn.

4th row 1ch to count as first dc, *3ch, now work 7tr into next 3ch sp between tr, 3ch, 1dc into 2nd of next 3dc at centre of shell, rep from * to end, working last dc into first ch of previous row. Turn.

5th row 1ch to count as first dc, 2ch, * 1dc into each of next 7tr of shell, 5ch, rep from * to last shell, 1dc into each of the 7tr in last shell, 2ch, 1dc into first ch of previous row. Turn.

6th row 3ch to count as first tr, 2ch, 1tr into first st at edge of work, *3ch, miss 2dc, 1dc into each of next 3dc at centre of shell, 3ch, (1tr, 3ch, 1tr) all into 3rd of next 5ch, rep from * to end, ending last rep by working (1tr, 2ch, 1tr) all into first ch of previous row. Turn.

The 1st to 6th rows form the pattern and are repeated throughout.

Lacy luxury

A delicate lace pattern and a soft fine yarn make this pretty evening cover-up. Wear it in the daytime, too, when you want a bit of extra warmth.

Size
Length when hanging, 90cm excluding fringe.

Materials
6 x 40g balls of Phildar Anouchka
3.50mm crochet hook

Tension
1 patt rep measures 5.5cm in width and 6cm in depth worked on 3.50mm hook.

To make
Make 244 ch very loosely.
Base row 3tr into 4th ch from hook, *miss next 3ch, 1dc into next ch, miss next 3ch, 7tr all into next ch, rep from * to end, but finish last rep 4tr into last ch instead of 7tr. Turn.
1st row 4ch, miss first tr, *1tr into next tr, 1ch, rep from * to end, finishing 1tr into turning ch. Turn.
2nd row 1ch, 1dc into first sp, 3ch, 1dc into next sp, 3ch, *miss next tr, 1dc into next tr, 1ch, 1dc into next tr, 3ch, miss next sp, (1dc into next sp, 3ch) 4 times, rep from * to within last 6 sps, miss next tr, 1dc into next tr, 1ch, 1dc into next tr, 3ch, miss next sp, 1dc into next sp, 3ch, 1dc into last sp. Turn.
3rd row Ss into first 3-ch sp, 3ch, 1dc into next 3-ch sp, *2ch, (1dc into next 3-ch sp, 3ch) 4 times, 1dc into next 3-ch sp, rep from * to end, finishing 2ch, 1dc into next 3-ch sp, 3ch, 1dc into last 3-ch sp. Turn.
4th row Ss into first 3-ch sp, *3ch, 1dc into next 3-ch sp, rep from * to end. Turn.
5th row *5ch, miss next 3-ch sp, (1dc into next 3-ch sp, 3ch) twice, 1dc into next 3-ch sp, rep from * to end, finishing 5ch, miss last 3-ch sp, 1dc into ss.

Turn.
6th row *7ch, 1dc into next 3-ch sp, 3ch, 1dc into next 3-ch sp, rep from * to end, finishing 7ch, 1dc into the last dc of the 4th row. Turn.
7th row Ss over the 7ch and into 3-ch sp, 3ch, 3tr into same sp, *2ch, 1dc into 4th of 7ch, 2ch, 7tr into 3-ch sp, rep from * to end, but finish last rep 4tr into last 3-ch sp instead of 7tr. Turn.
Rep rows 1 to 7 until patt remains, ending with a 6th row. Fasten off.

Fringe
Using four 30cm lengths of yarn together, knot fringe evenly along the two side edges. Trim the ends.

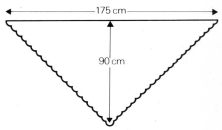

Brian Mayor

Step-by-step course – 26

*Hints on making up
*Blocking and pressing
*Sewing the pieces together
*Stitch Wise: diagonal shell pattern
*Pattern for a baby's jacket and bonnet

Hints on making up

Sooner or later – and probably sooner – you will crochet a garment which involves detailed making up. Many people think that once they have completed making all the separate pieces of a garment, the task is virtually finished, and that all they need to do is quickly sew the seams together. This, of course, is not true; careful pressing and seaming are essential if you want your garment to have a really professional finish. After all, you've probably spent a considerable amount of time and care in working the crochet. A few extra minutes at the making-up stage may well make the difference between a finished sweater, jacket or dress which you'll be proud to wear and one that stays in the cupboard.

Blocking and pressing

Where the pieces of your garment are to be pressed before seaming, you must first pin each piece out to the correct size and shape on a flat, padded surface. This is known as 'blocking'. Some yarns can be pressed, and some cannot. On most ball bands you will find pressing instructions using the international symbols, shown overleaf. The ball band should also tell you whether the yarn should be wet or dry pressed. Many man-made fibres need no pressing at all and can be ruined if they come into contact with heat, so check the ball band carefully before pressing. If you are in any doubt about how the yarn should be treated, it is better not to press it at all to avoid disappointment.

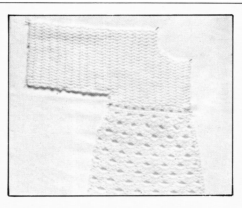

1 Place the piece to be pressed (RS down) on to a flat, well-padded surface. Your kitchen table covered with several layers of blankets and a sheet makes an ideal surface, since it is wider than an ordinary ironing board and provides plenty of room on which to lay the fabric out flat. Pin the piece at each corner as shown.

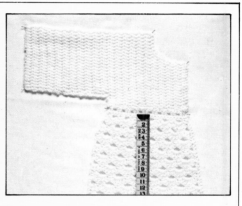

2 Now measure horizontally across the widest part and vertically down the centre of the fabric to make sure that the measurements are the same as those given in the instructions. If not, pat the fabric gently to the correct shape and size and pin once more at the lower edge.

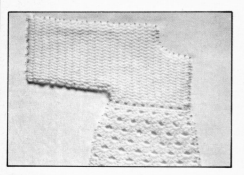

3 Now pin all round the fabric at intervals of about 2cm, taking care not to stretch the fabric, since this could result in a fluted edge. Check that each side measures the same and that stitches and rows are running straight before you begin to press.

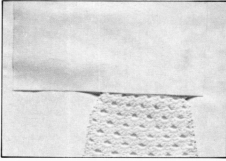

4 Place a clean, cotton cloth (either damp or dry depending on the type of yarn used) over the piece to be pressed. Remember that any ribbing on the garment should not be pressed, as this will flatten it, causing it to lose its elasticity.

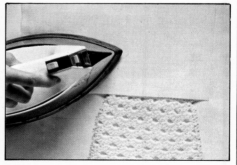

5 Pressing should always be done with a light touch, as over-pressing can easily ruin the soft, textured quality of crocheted fabrics. Set the iron at the correct temperature for the yarn, then press gently but firmly down on the cloth and lift the iron off again. Repeat this action all over the cloth, lifting and pressing, rather than pushing it over the cloth as when ironing. Allow the fabric to cool before removing the pins.

Fred Mancini

Special cases

Highly textured patterns, such as cluster patterns, are normally not pressed, for pressing may destroy their distinctive appearance. The same is generally true of lacy patterns. In some cases, however, (usually when a natural fibre has been used) the pattern will instruct you to press the garment lightly on the wrong side, taking care not to spoil the pattern. Block the garment over a folded towel and lay a damp cloth on top of it. Hold the iron so that it just touches the cloth and leave it there a second or so. Repeat over the whole surface of the piece – excluding ribbing, if any.

A lightly textured fabric may simply be blocked and pressed around the edges, as shown here.

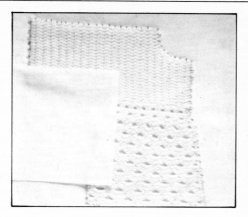

1 Block the piece to shape in the normal way, and then place a damp cloth over it.

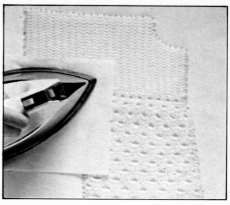

2 Press around the edges only. This creates a firm edge, making it easier to sew the pieces together. Allow the fabric to cool completely.

Ironing symbols

Iron with three dots: use a hot iron.

Iron with two dots: use a warm iron.

Iron with one dot: use a cool iron.

Iron with a cross through it: do not iron.

Sewing the pieces together

To sew crocheted fabrics together use a blunt-ended wool needle and the same yarn used for the garment. If this is too thick or unsuitable (a bouclé for example) you can substitute finer or more suitable yarn in a matching shade. Your instructions will usually tell you in which order the seams should be joined and the kind of seam to use for each piece. Remember that to avoid distorting the garment at the seams you must not draw the yarn too tightly through the fabric. Make sure that any patterns – such as shells or clusters – match exactly on each side of the seam before sewing the pieces together. You can, in some cases, use double crochet to join the pieces together. This is usually worked on the right side of the fabric with a contrasting coloured yarn to make a feature of the seam (See Crochet Course 4, page 11).

Back stitch seam

This seam is generally used for the main parts of the garment, such as shoulder, side and sleeve seams, on fabric that is closely woven or textured, such as double crochet, half treble or moss stitch fabrics. It creates a firm, strong seam ideal for sweaters and jackets.

1 Pin the two pieces to be joined with RS together. Work the seam approximately one crochet stitch in from the edge. Begin by making 2 small stitches on top of each other at the starting point of the seam to hold the yarn in place.

2 Insert the needle into the fabric again and bring it out slightly to the left of the fastening stitches. Now bring the needle to the right, insert it and bring it out a little farther to the left.

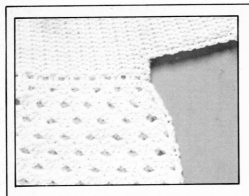
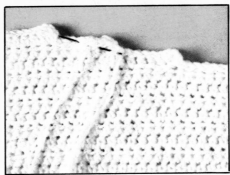
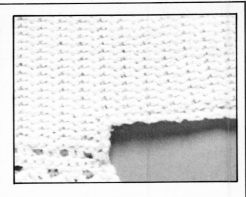

3 Continue to repeat step 2 all the way across the fabric, working in a straight line inserting the needle at the point where it emerged for the previous stitch, so that the stitches are all touching. Remember not to pull the yarn tightly.

4 If you are using this seam at the shoulder, work in a straight line from the outer (armhole) edge to the inner (neck) edge, rather than following the steps created by the shoulder shaping

5 If you had a set-in sleeve this could be sewn in first before joining the side and sleeve edges, these edges could then be joined in one continuous seam. This method produces a firm neat seam as shown here.

Oversewn seam

This is an ideal seam for ribbing or very open lace patterns, since it does not make a ridge on the fabric. The yarn is taken over the top of the edge and then passed through the edge stitches.

On lacy patterns, which may have more spaces than stitches along the edge – ruling out a back stitch seam – oversewing is a practical alternative, for you need only pass the needle through the centre of the chain or edge stitch to join the two pieces. Match any pattern on your fabric carefully on each side of the seam before joining the pieces together.

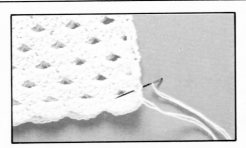
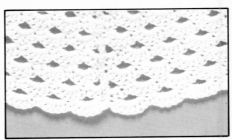

1 Place the two pieces with RS together. Using a blunt-ended needle and working from right to left make two small stitches at the beginning. With yarn at front of fabric pass the needle over the top of the two edges from front to back and insert the needle through the edges from back to front.

2 Now pull the yarn through firmly, but not too tightly, to complete the first stitch. Continue to work in same way across the fabric, working over the top across the fabric, working over the edges each time until the seam is complete.

Invisible seam

Here is another method of seaming which is also well-suited to very open lace crochet fabrics, since you can just catch the stitches at either side of the seam, rather than having to work through the double thickness of fabric each time. Because the seam lies perfectly flat, with no hard ridges, it is a also ideal for baby clothes, in which comfort is extremely important. Unlike the other seams it is worked with the pieces lying flat, RS upwards.

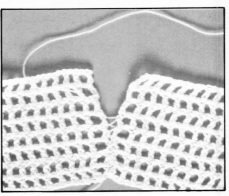

1 Place the two pieces of fabric edge to edge, RS facing upwards. Join the yarn on to one side of the seam, taking 2 small stitches to secure it. Now take the yarn over to the other side and pass the needle under one stitch. If the fabric is particularly fine, you can pass the needle under 1 loop only of the stitch.

2 Take the needle back to the other side and under the next stitch on this side in the same way. Pull the yarn through firmly so that the stitch becomes invisible. Continue to work along the seam, catching one stitch at either side until the seam has been completed.

Fred Mancini

Stitch Wise

Diagonal shell pattern

This pattern is worked over a multiple of 8 chain plus 7 extra chain, and shows how simple shells and chain links can be worked in diagonal, rather than vertical lines. Make sure that you work the base chain loosely.

Base row (RS) 1dc into 3rd ch from hook, *5ch, miss 3ch, 1dc into next ch, rep from * to end of ch. Turn.

1st row 3ch to count as first tr, 2tr into first (edge) dc – called half shell, 1dc into first 5ch loop, *5ch, 1dc into next 5ch loop, 5tr into next dc – called 1 shell, 1 dc into next 5ch loop, rep from * to end, ending last rep with 5ch, 1dc into top of turning chain. Turn.

2nd row 3ch to count as first tr, half shell into first dc, 1dc into next 5ch loop, *5ch, 1dc into centre tr of next shell, 1 shell into next dc, 1dc into next 5ch loop, rep from * ending last rep with 1dc into top of turning chain. Turn.

3rd row 6ch, 1dc into first 5ch loop, *1 shell into next dc, 1dc into centre tr of next shell, 5ch, 1 dc into next 5ch loop, rep from * to end, ending with 1 shell into last dc, 1dc into top of turning chain. Turn.

4th row 6ch, 1dc into centre tr of next shell, *1 shell into next dc, 1dc into next 5ch loop, 5ch, 1dc into centre of next shell, rep from *, ending with 1dc into centre tr of last shell, 1 shell into next dc, 1dc into 3rd of first 6ch. Turn.

5th row 3ch, half shell into first dc, 1dc into centre tr of next shell, *5ch, 1dc into next 5ch loop, 1 shell into next dc, 1dc into centre of next shell ; rep from * ending last rep with 5ch, 1dc into 3rd of first 6ch. Turn.

2nd to 5th rows form pattern and are repeated throughout.

For the little one

Make a jacket and matching bonnet for the newcomer in the family. The lacy pattern is highlighted by using a yarn with a shiny thread running through it producing a slightly lustrous effect.

Sizes
Jacket fits 46[48]cm chest.
Length, 28[30.5]cm.
Sleeve seam, 12[13.5]cm.

Note Instructions for the larger size are in square brackets [] ; where there is only one set of figures it applies to both sizes.

Materials
Jacket *5[6] x 20g balls of Emu Treasure Ripple Quickerknit*
3.50mm crochet hook
4.00mm crochet hook
3 buttons
1m of 1cm wide ribbon
Bonnet *2 balls of yarn as above*
3.50mm crochet hook
1m of 1.5cm-wide ribbon

Tension
22 sts to 10cm and 22 rows to 13cm over yoke patt on 3.50mm hook.

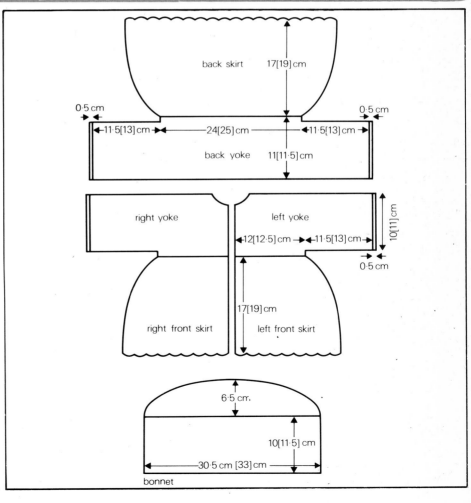

Jacket back yoke

Using 3.50mm hook make 23[26]ch for left cuff.

Base row (WS) 1 htr into 3rd ch from hook, 1 htr into each ch to end. Turn. 22[25] sts.
Commence patt.

1st row 2ch to count as first dc, working into *back* loops only, work 1dc into each st to end. Turn.

2nd row 2ch to count as first htr, 1 htr into each st to end. Turn.

Rep the last 2 rows until work measures 11.5[13]cm from beg, ending with a 2nd patt row.

Next row Work 4ch for underarm, 1dc in to 3rd ch from hook, 1dc into next ch, patt to end. Turn. 25[28] sts.

Cont in patt until work measures 35.5[38]cm from beg, ending with a 1st patt row.

Next row Patt to last 3 sts, turn and leave last 3 sts for underarm. 22[25] sts.

Cont in patt until work measures 47[51]cm from beg, ending with a 1st patt row. Fasten off.

Left front yoke

Work as given for back yoke until front measures 1 row less than back yoke to first underarm, so ending with a 1st patt row. Fasten off.

Shape underarm

Next row Work 3ch, then patt across sts of sleeve. Turn.

Next row Patt across 22[25] sts, 1dc into each of next 3ch. Turn. 25[28] sts.

Cont in patt over all sts until front measures 7.5[9]cm from underarm, ending with a 1st patt row.

Shape neck

Next row Patt to last 5[6] sts, turn.

Dec one st at neck edge on next 3 rows. 17[19] sts. Work 4 rows without shaping. Fasten off.

Right front yoke

Using 3.50mm hook make 18[20]ch.
Work base row as given for back yoke. 17[19] sts.

Next row (buttonhole row) 2ch, patt 1[2] sts, (2ch, miss 2 sts, patt 3 sts) 3 times, patt 0[1].

Work 2 rows in patt, then inc one st at neck edge on next 3 rows, so ending with a 2nd patt row. Fasten off.

Shape neck

Next row Work 5[6]ch, patt across sts of front. Turn.

Next row Patt to last 5[6]ch, 1htr into each of next 5[6]ch. Turn. 25[28] sts.

Cont in patt until front measures 7.5[9]cm from end of neck shaping, ending with a 1st patt row. Fasten off.

Next row Miss first 3 sts for underarm, rejoin yarn to next st, 2ch, patt to end. Turn. 22[25] sts.

Cont in patt until front measures 11.5[13]cm from underarm, ending with a 1st patt row. Fasten off.

Back skirt

Using 3.50mm hook and with RS of work facing, work 50[56]dc across lower edge of back yoke. Turn.

Next row (eyelet-hole row) 2ch, 1htr into next st, *1ch, miss next st, 1htr into each of next 2 sts, rep from * to end. Turn.

Next row 2ch, 1dc into each htr and ch of previous row. Turn. 50[56]dc. Change to 4.00mm hook. Commence patt.**

1st size only

Base row 2ch, 1dc into next st, *3ch, miss next st, 1dc into each of next 3 sts, rep from * to last 4 sts, 3ch, 1dc into each of last 2 sts. Turn.

2nd size only

Base row 2ch, 1dc into first st, *3ch, miss next st, 1dc into each of next 3 sts, rep from * to last 3 sts, 3ch, miss next st, 1dc into each of last 2 sts. Turn.

Both sizes

***1st row** 2ch, 1dc into next st, *5tr into 3ch sp, 1dc into centre dc of 3dc, rep from * to end, finishing with 1dc into last st. Turn.

2nd row 2ch, *3ch, 1dc into each of centre 3tr of group, rep from * to end, finishing with 2ch, 1tr into last st. Turn.

3rd row 3ch, 2tr into 2ch sp, *1dc into centre dc of 3dc, 5tr into 3ch sp, rep from * to end, finishing with 2tr into 3ch sp, 1tr into last st. Turn.

4th row 2ch, 1dc into next tr, *3ch, 1dc into each of centre 3tr of group, rep from * to end, finishing with 3ch, 1dc into each of last 2sts. Turn.

The last 4 rows form the patt. Rep them 4 times more.

1st size only

Rep 1st row once more. Fasten off.

2nd size only

Rep 1st-3rd rows inclusive once more. Fasten off.

Right front skirt

Using 3.50mm hook and with RS of work facing, work 26[29]dc across lower edge of right front yoke. Work as given for back skirt from ** to **.

1st size only

Base row Work as given for back.

2nd size only

Base row 2ch, 1dc into next st, *3ch, miss next st, 1dc into each of next 3 sts, rep from * to last 3 sts, 3ch, miss next st, 1dc into each of last 2 sts. Turn.

Both sizes

Work as given for back skirt from *** to end.

Left front skirt

Work as given for right front skirt.

To make up

Press lightly on WS using a cool iron over dry cloth. Join shoulder and upper sleeve seams, then skirt and underarm seams. **Front and neck edging** Using 3.50mm hook and with RS of work facing, work 1 row of dc up right front, round neck edge and down left front, working 3dc into each corner. Fasten off.

Using 3.50mm hook and with RS of work facing, rejoin yarn to top of right front and work round neck edge as foll : 1ch, *1dc into each of next 2 sts, 3ch, ss into first ch – picot formed, 1dc into next st, rep from * to top of left front. Fasten off.

Cuff edging Using 3.50mm hook and with RS of work facing, work 36[42]dc round cuff edge. Join with a ss into first dc.

2nd round Work in dc, dec 6 sts evenly.

3rd round Work picots as given for neck edging. Fasten off.

Sew on buttons to correspond with buttonholes. Thread ribbon through eyelet holes to tie at front.

Bonnet

Using 3.50mm hook make 68[74]ch. Work base row and patt 3 rows as given for jacket back yoke. 67[73] sts. Commence patt.

Base row 2ch, 1dc into next st, *3ch, miss 3 sts, 1dc into each of next 3 sts, rep from * to last 5 sts, 3ch, miss 3 sts, 1dc into each of last 2 sts. Turn.

Cont in patt as given for back skirt until bonnet measures 10[11.5]cm from beg, ending with a 2nd or 4th patt row.

Next row 1ch, 1dc into each dc and ch of previous row. Turn.

Work 3 more rows in dc.

Shape crown

1st row 2ch, 1dc into each of next 0[3]sts, (1dc into each of next 15 sts, work 2dc tog) 3 times, 1dc into each of next 15[18] sts. Turn. 64[70] sts.

2nd and every alt row 1ch, 1dc into each st of previous row. Turn.

3rd row 2ch, 1dc into each of next 0[3] sts, (1dc into each of next 7 sts, work 2dc tog) 7 times, 1dc into each of next 0[3] sts. Turn. 57[63] sts.

5th row 2ch, 1dc into each of next 0[3] sts, (1dc into each of next 6 sts, work 2dc tog) 7 times, 1dc into each of next 0[3] sts. Turn. 50[56] sts.

7th row 2ch, 1dc into each of next 0[3] sts, (1dc into each of next 5 sts, work 2dc tog) 7 times, 1dc into each of next 0[3] sts. Turn. 43[49] sts.

Cont to dec in this way on every alt row until 8[14] sts rem.

2nd size only

Next row (Work 2dc tog) 7 times.

Both sizes

Cut yarn, thread through rem 8[7] sts, draw up and fasten off securely.

To make up

Press as given for jacket. Join seam as far as start of crown shaping.

Edging Using 3.50mm hook and with RS of work facing, work one round of dc round front and neck edges. Fasten off.

Cut ribbon in half ; make a rosette at one end of each length and sew to bonnet as shown.

Step-by-step course – 27

Working cluster or bobble stitches

Cluster stitches – or bobble stitches as they are sometimes called – can be grouped together to form diamond or square shapes on a plain background, or incorporated into square, flat motifs, or used as an all-over pattern to produce a really chunky crochet fabric. There are various ways of making these stitches. The preferred method depends largely on the type of stitch being used for the background and on the kind of texture desired. Relatively few stitches, grouped together and interspersed with other stitches, will produce a softly textured fabric. Other techniques will produce large bobbles that stand out against the fabric, giving it a highly embossed appearance.

All kinds of cluster stitches are made in essentially the same way : by working a number of loops or stitches into the same place and then drawing them together with a chain to complete the group. In a pattern containing cluster stitches, the instructions will specify the particular method of working the clusters for that garment.

Making a simple cluster group

This is a simple stitch to work ; all you do is draw a number of loops through one stitch in the previous row, then draw the yarn through all the loops, gathering them together. The width of each cluster will tend to make a row of these stitches wider than the rest of the fabric. If you are working bands of clusters in a plain fabric, you should insert a row of double crochet between each two cluster rows to control the extra fullness and maintain the shape of the fabric.

1 Work at least 2 treble at the beginning of the row where the cluster is to be made. This will be the RS of the fabric. Wind the yarn round the hook and insert the hook into the next stitch. Draw through a length of yarn, pulling it up to approximately 15mm, or so it is the same height as the previous stitch. There are now 3 loops on the hook.

2 Wind the yarn round the hook and insert it into the same stitch as before. Now draw up another loop so that it is the same height as the first loop. There are now 5 loops on the hook.

3 Repeat step 2 twice more, so that there are now 9 loops on the hook. The number of times you repeat this step will depend on the size of bobble or cluster you wish to make.

4 Now wind yarn round the hook and draw it through all the loops on the hook to complete the cluster. Make 1 chain to hold the stitches firmly together.

5 Work at least 1 treble between each cluster all the way across the row and 2 treble after the last group to keep the edge straight. This sample shows several rows worked with 1 double crochet row between each cluster row. Work a double crochet into each treble and into the top of each cluster on the double crochet rows to maintain the number of stitches.

Paul Williams

Raised bobbles

The following method produces firm, raised bobbles made of trebles worked against a background of double crochet. You can work these bobbles to make an all-over pattern or group them into diamond or square shapes on a plain background. You will need to work at least 2 rows in double crochet before making the bobbles.

1 Work at least 2 double crochet at the beginning of the row. Now work 5 treble into the next stitch in the row below (placing the hook into the centre of the stitch), drawing the yarn up each time to the same height as the stitches in the row being worked.

2 Remove the hook from the working loop and insert it under the two horizontal loops of the first of these 5 treble. Take care not to pull the working loop back through the last stitch when withdrawing the hook.

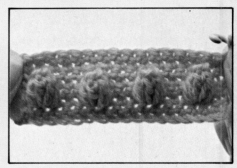

3 Now insert the hook once more into the working loop, so that the first treble and last treble of the group are both on the hook at the same time and the hook passes behind the 5 treble.

4 Draw the working loop through the first of these loops to complete the bobble. Make 1 chain to hold the stitches just worked firmly together.

5 Continue to work bobbles across the row ; miss the next stitch (the stitch missed in this row when 5 treble were worked into the row below) then work 1 double crochet into each of the next 3 stitches before making the next bobble in the same way as before. Finish the row by working at least 1 or 2 double crochet after the last bobble.

Pineapple stitch

This is a classic crochet cluster stitch in which loops are drawn through the vertical strand at the side of each group to make a horizontal rather than a vertical cluster. Pineapple stitch makes an ideal edging for a jacket or cardigan.
You will need to work at least one row in double crochet or trebles before working the cluster row, and you must have an even number of stitches on which to work it.

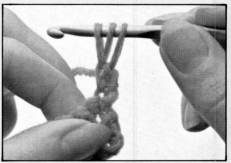

1 Work 2 chain at the beginning of the cluster row to keep the edge straight. Work a double crochet into the first (edge) stitch and then 1 chain. Now draw this chain (working loop) out loosely so that it is about 15mm long.

2 Wind the yarn round hook and insert the hook from front to back into the vertical loop at the side of the last stitch. Now draw through a loop loosely, extending it to the same height as before (3 loops on hook).

Paul Williams

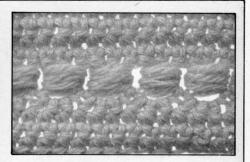

3 Repeat step 2 three times more (9 loops on hook). Pull each loop through loosely to prevent the cluster from becoming distorted. Miss next 2 double crochet. Insert hook into next stitch ; wind yarn round hook and draw it through this stitch and all loops on hook to complete first cluster.

4 To make the next cluster make 2 chain, drawing 2nd chain out to 15mm as before. Wind the yarn round hook and insert it from front to back into vertical loop at side of the last cluster into the loop made when first chain was worked after last cluster.

5 Complete this cluster as before. Make each cluster in the same way, inserting hook each time into vertical loop at side of last cluster worked. Finish the row with 1 chain and 1 treble into turning chain. For the next row, work 3 double crochet under top 2 loops of each cluster and 1 double crochet at each end.

Stitch Wise

Cluster stitch motif

Cluster groups worked in rounds have been used to make this highly textured square motif. You can make it in a fine or chunky yarn using either one colour, or changing the colour of the yarn at the end of each round for a really colourful effect.

Make 6ch and join into a circle with a slip stitch.

1st round 2ch to count as first dc, work 15dc into circle. Join with a ss to 2nd of first 2ch. 16dc.

2nd round 4ch to count as first cluster and 1 ch sp, *yrh and insert hook into next st, yrh and draw through a loop, yrh and draw through all 3 loops, called Cl1, 1 ch, rep from * to end of round. Join last ch to 3rd of first 4ch with a ss. 16 clusters.

3rd round Ss into first ch sp, 3ch, (yrh and insert hook into same sp, yrh and draw through a loop) twice, yrh and draw through all loops on hook, 2ch, * (yrh and insert hook into next 1 ch sp, yrh and draw through a loop) 3 times, yrh and draw through all loops on hook, called Cl3, 2ch, rep from * to end of round. Ss into 3rd of first 3ch.

4th round Ss into first 2ch sp, 3ch to count as first tr, 1tr into same sp, (2tr into next 2ch sp, 1ch) twice, 1ch (Cl3, 2ch, Cl3) into next 2ch sp, called corner group, 1ch, *(2tr into next 2ch sp, 1ch) 3 times, 1 corner group into next 2ch sp, rep from * to end of round, working last corner group into sp before first 3ch in previous round and joining last ch to 3rd of first 3ch with a ss. Fasten off.

All-over cluster pattern

Several loops are worked into one stitch in the row below to create this really chunky cluster pattern. It may be substituted for the raised bobbles opposite. Make a number of chain divisible by 4 plus 1, with 1 extra for turning chain.

1st row (RS) 1dc into 3rd ch from hook, 1dc into each ch to end. Turn.

2nd row 1ch to count as first dc, miss first 1dc, 1dc into each dc to end, working last dc into turning chain. Turn.

3rd row 1ch, miss first dc, 1dc into next dc, *(yrh, insert hook into st in row below next dc, yrh and draw a loop through, extending it to the height of row being worked) 5 times, yrh and draw a loop through, extending it to height of row, 1 ch, called Cl1, miss next dc (this is the dc missed when cluster was worked into row below), 1 dc into next dc, rep from * to end. 1 dc into turning chain. Turn.

4th row 1ch, miss first dc, 1dc into next dc, *1dc into top of next cluster, 1dc into dc between clusters, rep from * to last cluster, 1dc into top of last cluster, 1dc into next dc, 1dc into turning chain. Turn.

5th row 1ch, miss first dc, *Cl1 into next st in row below next dc, miss next dc (dc missed in this row when cluster was worked in row below), 1dc into next dc, rep from * to last 2dc, Cl1 into next dc, 1dc into turning chain. Turn.

6th row 1ch, *1dc into top of cluster, 1dc into next dc between clusters, rep from * to last cluster, 1dc into top of last cluster, 1dc into turning chain. Turn.

3rd to 6th rows form pattern.

Kim Sayer

Soft clusters

This classic slipover made in a mohair-type yarn has bands of cluster stitches which give it an embossed look.

Sizes
To fit 82/87[92/97] cm bust.
Length, 57[62]cm.

Note Instructions for larger size are in square brackets []; where there is only one set of figures it applies to both sizes.

Materials
5[6] x 50g balls of Pingouin
   Poudreuse
4.50mm and 5.50mm crochet hooks

Tension
6 clusters and 10 rows to 10cm over patt worked on 5.50mm hook.

Back
**Using 4.50mm hook make 13ch for side edge of welt.
Base row 1dc into 3rd ch from hook, 1dc into each ch to end. Turn.
Next row 2ch to count as first dc, miss first st, *1dc into back loop only of next st, rep from * to end, working last st into back loop of turning ch. Turn. 12dc.
Rep last row 54[58] times more. This completes the ribbing for the welt.

Do not turn but continue to work down the long side edge of the ribbing. Change to 5.50mm hook. Working into the row ends, work 59[63] dc evenly along this edge. Turn.
Next row 2ch to count as first dc, 1dc into each dc to end. Turn. 59[63] dc. Commence patt.
1st row 4ch to count as first tr and 1ch, miss next dc, yrh, insert hook into next dc, yrh and draw a loop through, (yrh, insert hook into same dc, yrh and draw a loop through) 3 times, yrh and draw through all loops on hook, called Cl1, *1ch, miss next dc, 1 cluster into next dc, 1ch, miss next dc, rep from * to end, finishing 1ch, miss next dc, 1tr into turning ch. Turn. 28[30] clusters.
2nd row 2ch, *1dc into next ch, 1dc into top of next cluster, rep from * to end, finishing 1dc into each of next 2ch. Turn. 59[63] dc.
3rd row 2ch, 1dc into each dc to end. Turn.
These 3 rows form the patt. Cont in patt until back measures 32[35]cm from beg, ending with a 3rd patt row.**

Shape armholes
Next row Ss over first 9dc, 4ch, *miss next dc, Cl1 into next dc, 1ch, rep from * until 20[22] clusters in all have been worked, 1ch, miss next dc, 1tr into next dc, turn and leave rem sts unworked.
Cont in patt as set, working 43[47]sts in each dc row, until back measures 24[27]cm from beg of armhole shaping, ending with a 2nd patt row.

Shape shoulders
1st row Ss over first 8sts, patt to within last 7sts, turn.
2nd row Patt to end. Turn.
3rd row Ss over first 7sts, patt to within last 6sts. Fasten off.

Front
Work as given for back from ** to **.

Shape armhole and divide for neck
Next row Ss over first 9dc, work in patt until 10[11] clusters in all have been worked, turn and leave rem sts.
1st row Patt to end. Turn. 21[23] dc.
2nd row Patt to within last 3dc, work next 2dc tog to dec one st, 1dc into last dc. Turn. 20[22] dc.
3rd row 3ch, Cl1 into next dc, patt to end. Turn. 9[10] clusters.
4th row Patt to end. Turn.
5th row 2ch, dec one dc, patt to end. Turn.
6th row Patt to end. Turn.
Rep these 6 rows until 6 clusters rem, ending with a cluster row.

Shape shoulder
Next row Work 7[8]dc. Fasten off.
Return to rem sts. With RS of work facing, miss next dc, rejoin yarn to next st, Cl1, cont in patt until 10[11] clusters have been worked in all, 1ch, miss next dc, 1tr into next dc, turn and leave rem sts for armhole. Complete to match first side reversing shaping.

To make up
Join shoulder seams.
Neck border
With RS of left front facing and using 4.50mm hook, rejoin yarn to neck edge and work 33[37]dc down left front neck, miss centre st, work 33[37]dc up right front neck and 16[17]dc across back neck. Join with a ss to first dc. 82[91]dc. Working into back loop only, work 3 rounds in dc, dec 2sts at centre on each round by working 3dc tog at point of V on every round. Fasten off.
Armhole borders (alike)
Join side seams. With RS of work facing join yarn to underarm and using 4.50mm hook work 1dc into each st along underarm, then work in dc round armhole working 2dc into each cluster row end and 1dc for every 2dc row ends, then work 1dc into each st along underarm. Join with a ss to first dc. Working into back loop only, work 1 round in dc, ss into first dc.
Next round Work 7dc, now work 2dc tog to dec one st, work 1dc into each dc all round armhole to within last 10dc, work next 2dc tog, work to end, ss into first dc.
Next round 1dc into each of first 6dc, work next 2dc tog, 1dc into each dc to within last 9dc, work next 2dc tog, 1dc into each dc to end. Fasten off.

Diagram labels

BACK

35 [37] cm

6 cm

FRONT

46 [49] cm

25 [27] cm

49 [54] cm

8 cm

John Hutchinson

Step-by-step course – 28

*Shell fabric pattern
*Eyelet lace pattern
*Mother and daughter patterns : woman's shirt and girl's tunic.

Shell fabric pattern

This very simple shell stitch pattern has been used for the woman's shirt and the girl's tunic featured in this course. It has a slightly textured appearance without being too bulky. Because the pattern consists of two stitches worked into one, making a fan shaped group, it is important to work the foundation chain as loosely as possible.

Before making one of the garments in this course, make a sample to check your tension and see the over-all effect. If necessary, work the foundation chain with a larger hook than the one used for the pattern.

As you can see from the girl's tunic, it is possible to work bands of colour by introducing new colours at the end of a row. We worked one row in the first contrasting colour, followed by three rows in a second contrasting colour. The pattern is worked over an even number of stitches. We have made 25 chain and worked the first double crochet into the 3rd chain from the hook, so that there are 24 double crochet in the first row of the sample.

1 On the 1st row of this pattern you will not need to work any turning chain, since the first shell group is worked at the edge of the fabric. Begin by working a double crochet, chain and treble all into the 2nd stitch to form the first graduated shell.

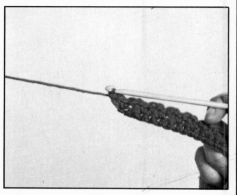

2 Now miss the next double crochet and work another group into the next stitch. Continue to work a group in the same way into every other stitch all the way across the row, working the last group into the top of the turning chain to complete the row.

3 Now turn the work and make 2 chain. From this point on, a turning chain is required at the beginning of every row. Miss the first treble and 1-chain space and work a group in the same way as before into the next double crochet. (This is the double crochet worked at the beginning of the last group in the previous row.)

4 Continue to work a group in the same way into each double crochet worked in the previous row until you reach the end of the row. The last group should be worked into the edge of the fabric this time, since there is no turning chain.

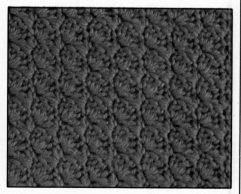

5 To continue the pattern, repeat the 2nd row each time, remembering that the last group should be worked into the top of the turning chain on subsequent rows.

Eyelet lace pattern

This fabric has a slightly lacy look and could be used for a summer blouse or an evening top. The pattern is worked over a multiple of 6 chain plus 3 extra. Our sample requires 27 chain in all, and is worked in a double knitting yarn with a 4.50mm hook, although this pattern looks equally good worked in a finer ply or a cotton yarn.

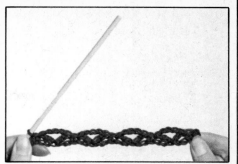

1 Work a double crochet into the 3rd chain from the hook. Now miss the next 2 chain and work 1 treble, followed by 3 chain and 1 treble, all into the next chain to create the first V-shaped group. Now miss the next 2 chain and work a double crochet into the following chain.

2 Continue to work a V group and a double crochet alternately across the row into every 3rd chain, completing the row by working a double crochet into the last chain. The pattern consists of these two simple steps worked alternately, reversing their position on every row.

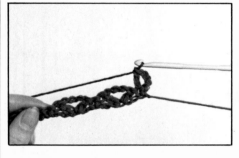

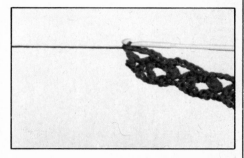

3 To keep the edge of the fabric straight and the pattern running in the correct sequence, you will have to work a half V at the beginning of the next row. This is done by working 4 chain to count as the first treble into the first stitch to complete the group. Thus the half group is achieved by working 1 chain in the middle of the 2 trebles instead of 3.

4 Now work a double crochet into the next 3-chain loop at the centre of the first V group, followed by a V group into the double crochet between the first two V groups worked in the previous row.

5 Continue to work a double crochet and a V group alternately across the row, completing the row by working a half V group consisting of 1 treble, 1 chain and 1 treble, all worked into the top of the turning chain.

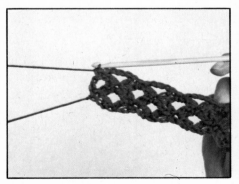

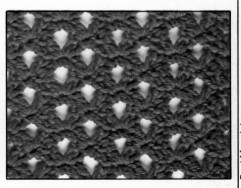

6 Begin the next row with 1 chain and then work a double crochet into the chain space in the centre of the first half V group at the edge of the work.

7 Now work a V group as before into the double crochet between the first and 2nd V groups in the previous row, thus reversing the pattern once more. Continue to work a V group and double crochet alternately across the row, finishing by working a double crochet into the 3rd of the first 4 chain, thus leaving the 4th of these chain to count as the 1-chain space in the V group of the previous row.

8 The all-over eyelet effect is created by alternating the rows in this way for the pattern, beginning one row with a half V group and the next with a double crochet.

Fred Mancini

Mother and daughter duo

A beautifully casual pair for mother and daughter, worked in a shell stitch fabric and trimmed with crochet-covered buttons. The girl's dress follows the lines of the shirt-style sweater, but has bands of colour across the chest.

Victor Yuan

Woman's shirt

Sizes
To fit 87 [92 :97] cm bust.
Length, 64[66 :68]cm.
Sleeve seam, 43[44 :45]cm.
Note Instructions for larger sizes are in square brackets [] ; where there is only one set of figures it applies to all sizes.

Materials
9[10 :11] x 50g balls of Pingouin Confortable Fin
3.00mm and 3.50mm crochet hooks
Cotton-wool for buttons

Tension
7½ groups and 18 rows to 10cm on 3.50mm hook.

Back
Using 3.50mm hook make 80 [84 :88] ch very loosely.
Base row 1 dc into 3rd ch from hook, 1 dc into each ch to end. Turn. 79[83 :87] sts. Cut off yarn and turn.
Shape lower edge
1st row Miss 24dc, rejoin yarn to next dc, 1 ch, (1dc, 1 ch, 1tr) ito next dc – called 1 group or 1gr – (miss next dc, 1gr into next dc) 14[16 :18] times, 1dc into next dc, turn (leaving 24 sts unused at end).
2nd row 2ch, miss first dc, (1gr into dc of next gr) 15[17 :19] times, ss into 1 ch at beg of 1st row, (miss next dc, 1gr into next dc) twice, 1dc into next dc, turn (thus using 5 of the dc which were left at beg of 1st row).
3rd row 2ch, miss first dc, (1gr into dc of next gr) 17[19 :21] times, ss into 2ch at beg of last row, (miss next dc, 1gr into next dc) twice, 1dc into next dc, turn. Working 2 more gr on each row, rep the 3rd row 6 times more.
10th row 2ch, miss first dc, (1gr into dc of next gr) 31 [33 :35] times, ss into 2ch at beg of last row, (miss next dc, 1gr into next dc) twice, turn.
11th row 1 ch, (1gr into dc of next gr) 33[35 :37] times, ss into 2ch at beg of last row, (miss next dc, 1gr into next dc) twice, turn. 35[37 :39]gr.
You should now have used up all the dc which were left spare at the beginning, having used 5dc at the end of every row until the last 2 rows and 4 at the end of last 2 rows.
12th row 1 ch, 1gr into dc of each gr to end. Turn.
Rep the 12th row until work measures 45cm from beg, (measured at centre).
Shape armholes
Next row Ss over 2gr, 1 ch, patt to within last 2gr, turn.
Next row Patt to end. Turn.
Next row Ss over first gr, 1 ch, patt to within last gr, turn.
Rep the last 2 rows twice more. 25[27 : 29]gr. Cont without shaping until armholes measure 19[21 :23]cm.

Shape shoulders
Next row Ss over 2gr, patt to within last 2gr, turn.
Next row Ss over 2[3 :3]gr, patt to within last 2[3 :3]gr, turn.
Next row Ss over 3gr, patt to within last 3gr. Fasten off.

Front
Work as given for back until work measures 35cm from beg.
Divide for front opening
Next row Work 17[18 :19]gr, turn and cont on these sts until work measures the same as back to armholes, ending at side.
Shape armhole
Next row Ss over 2gr, 1 ch, patt to end. Turn.
Next row Patt to end. Turn.
Next row Ss over first gr, patt to end. Turn.
Rep the last 2 rows twice more. 12[13 : 14] gr. Cont without shaping until armhole measures 14 [16 :18] cm, ending at armhole edge.
Shape neck
Next row Patt to within last 2[2 :3]gr, turn.
Next row Patt to end. Turn.
Next row Patt to within last gr, turn.
Rep the last 2 rows twice more, then cont on rem 7[8 :8]gr until armhole measures the same as back armholes ending at armhole edge.
Shape shoulder
Next row Ss over 2gr, patt to end. Turn.
Next row Patt to within last 2[2 :3]gr, turn.
Next row Ss over 3gr, patt to end. Fasten off.
Return to where work was left, rejoin yarn to next dc, 1 ch, 1gr into next dc, patt to end. Turn. 17[18 :19]gr.

Complete to match first side, reversing shaping.

Sleeves
Using 3.50mm hook make 51 [55 :59]ch.
Base row 1dc into 3rd ch from hook, 1dc into each ch to end. Turn. 50[54 :58] sts.
1st row 1 ch, miss first dc, 1gr into next dc, *miss next dc, 1gr into next dc, rep from * to end. Turn. 25[27 :29]gr.
2nd row 1 ch, 1gr into dc of each gr to end. Rep the 2nd row until work measures 43[44 :45]cm from beg.
Shape top
Next row Ss over first gr, 1 ch, patt to within last 2gr, turn.
Rep the last row 7[8 :9] times more. Fasten off.

Cuffs (make 2)
Using 3.00mm hook make 7ch.
Base row 1dc into 3rd ch from hook, 1dc into each dc to end. Turn. 6 sts.
Next row 2ch to count as first dc, 1dc into each dc to end. Turn.
Rep last row until cuff measures 18[19 : 20]cm. Fasten off.

Collar
Using 3.00mm hook make 13ch and work base row as given for cuffs. 12dc. Cont in dc for 36[38 :40]cm. Fasten off.

To make up
Do not press. Join the shoulder seams. Sew in sleeves, sewing the last 2cm of sleeve seams to the first 2gr of armhole. Join side and sleeve seams, leaving sleeve seams open for about 7cm from lower edge. Sew on cuffs, gathering sleeve edge to fit. Sew on collar

Brian Mayor

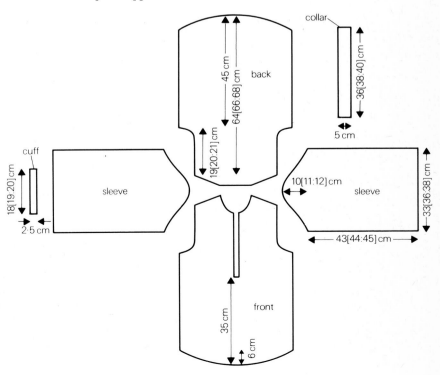

Front fastening

Starting at top of left front collar work 1 row of dc round front opening. Turn. Work another row of dc all round, making eight 5-chain buttonloops, first to come at neck edge and 7 evenly spaced down right front. Make 8 cotton-wool crochet buttons and sew to left front to match loops.

Child's tunic

Victor Yuan

Brian Mayor

Sizes
To fit 56[61:66]cm chest.
Length, 46[51:56]cm.
Sleeve seam, 22[24:26]cm.

Note Instructions for larger sizes are in square brackets [] ; where there is only one set of figures it applies to all sizes.

Materials
4[4:5] x 50g balls of Pingouin
  Confortable Fin in main colour (A)
1 ball in each of 2 contrasting colours
  (B) and (C)
3.00mm and 3.50mm crochet hooks
Cotton-wool for buttons

Tension
7½ groups and 18 rows to 10cm on 3.50mm hook.

Back
Using 3.50mm hook and A, make 51[55:59]ch.
Base row 1dc into 3rd ch from hook, 1dc into each ch to end. Turn.
1st row 1ch, miss first dc, (1dc, 1ch and 1tr) into next dc – called 1 group or 1gr, *miss next dc, 1gr into next dc, rep from * to end. Turn. 25[27:29]gr.
2nd row 1ch, 1gr into dc of each gr to end. Turn.
Rep the 2nd row until work measures 33[37:41]cm from beg.
Shape armholes
Next row Ss over 2gr, 1ch, patt to within last 2gr, turn.
Next row Patt to end. Turn.
Next row Ss over first gr, 1ch, patt to within last gr, turn.
Rep the last 2 rows once more. Now work 1[3:5] rows without shaping. Cut off A.
Join on B. With B work 2 rows.
Join on C. With C work 6 rows.
With B work 2 rows. Cut off B.
Cont with C until armholes measure 13[14:15]cm.
Fasten off.

Front
Work as given for back until work measures 28[32:36]cm from beg.
Divide for front opening
Next row Patt over 12[13:14]gr, turn and cont on these sts until work measures the same as back to beg of armhole shaping, ending at side edge.
Shape armhole
Next row Ss over 2gr, 1ch, patt to end. Turn.
Next row Patt to end. Turn.
Next row Ss over first gr, 1ch, patt to end. Turn.
Rep the last 2 rows once more. Now work 1[3:5] rows without shaping.
Cont in stripes to match back until armhole measures 9[10:11]cm, ending at armhole edge.
Shape neck
Next row Patt to within last 2gr, turn.
Next row Patt to end. Turn.
Next row Patt to within last gr, turn.
For 3rd size only, rep the last 2 rows once more.
For all sizes, cont without shaping until armhole measures same as back. Fasten off.
Return to where sts were left, rejoin yarn to next dc, 1ch, 1gr into next dc, patt to end. Turn.
Complete to match first side, reversing shaping.

Sleeves
Using 3.50mm hook and A, make 31[35:39]ch. Work base row as given for back. 15[17:19] gr.
Cont in patt as given for back until sleeve measures 22[24:26]cm from beg.
Shape top
Next row Ss over first gr, 1ch, patt to within last gr, turn.
Rep this row 4[5:6] times. Fasten off.

Cuffs
Using 3.00mm hook and B, make 6ch.
Base row 1dc into 3rd ch from hook, 1dc into each dc to end. Turn. 5sts.
Next row 2ch to count as first dc, 1dc into each dc to end. Turn.
Rep last row until cuff measures 15[16:17]cm. Fasten off.

Collar
Using 3.00mm hook and B, make 11ch and work base row as given for cuffs. 10dc. Cont in dc for 26[28:30]cm. Fasten off.

To make up
See women's shirt.

Front fastening
Using B, work front edging as given for mother's shirt, making six 5-chain buttonloops on right front.
Using C, make six small cotton-wool crochet buttons (see page 759), and sew to left front to match loops.

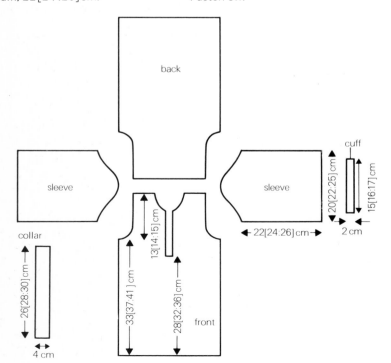

Step-by-step course – 29

Three-dimensional flower motifs

In this course we show you one of the most intriguing and unusual crochet techniques : working a three-dimensional flower motif. The flowers are most frequently worked as part of a crochet square such as the granny square featured in Crochet Course 14 (page 55). but they can, of course, be worked as separate motifs and sewn on to any crocheted or knitted fabric or on to clothes, as well.

Today, these flowers are usually worked in a knitting yarn or fairly thick cotton, and used to decorate bedspreads, rugs or elaborate shawls ; but in the past they were more often worked with a fine steel crochet hook in very fine crochet cotton and used on baby clothes, lingerie and fine lace collars. Such very fine crochet was particularly fashionable in the middle and late 19th century, when people were accustomed to spending long hours patiently doing intricate needlework.

Crocheted rose

These step-by-step instructions show you how to work the beautiful rose featured on the bedspread at the end of this course. In our sample – as in the bedspread pattern – each 2 layers of petals are worked in a different colour, but you could, of course, use just one colour.

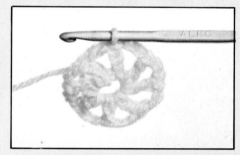

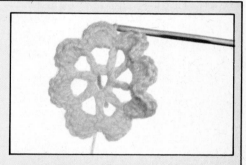

1 Begin the flower with 6 chain ; join them into a circle with a slip stitch. The first round is made by working 1 treble and 2 chain into the circle 8 times in all, thus making the 8 centre 'ribs' of the flower. First, make 5 chain ; these chain will count as the first treble and 2 chain space. Continue to work 1 treble and 2 chain around the circle, 7 more times. Finish the round by joining the last chain to the 3rd of the 5 chain with a slip stitch.

2 For the second round work 1 double crochet, 1 half treble, 3 trebles, 1 half treble and 1 double crochet into each 2-chain space of the previous round. Each of these groups of stitches forms a petal. Complete the round by using a slip stitch to join the last stitch to the slip stitch worked at the end of the previous round.

3 The next round consists of chains linking the petals already worked ; the chains are joined to the petals with double crochet. Begin by making 4 chain. Now insert the hook from back to front and round the stem of the first treble worked in the 1st round and work a double crochet in the normal way.

4 Keeping the 4 chain at the back of the petals all the time, work 4 chain and then a double crochet round the next treble in the first round all the way round the flower. Complete the round by working 4 chain and joining this with a slip stitch to the first chain at the beginning of the previous round.

5 Some patterns instruct you to turn the flower so the WS faces you when working the chains. In this case work the double crochet round the stem of the stitch worked in the previous round, then turn flower to RS again before you work the petals. Here we show the back of the flower with linking chains worked in a contrast colour.

continued

Fred Mancini

6 Now work a petal into each of the chain loops worked in the previous round. You should work 5 treble instead of the 3 worked in the previous petal round to increase the size of these petals. Use a slip stitch to join the last double crochet of the last petal to the first. You will see that the flower now has two layers.

7 Now work chain loops in exactly the same way as for the 3rd round, but work the double crochet linking each 4 chain loop round the back of the double crochet which you worked in the 3rd round. This has the effect of pulling the flower together at the back.

8 Work another round of petals into these chain loops as before, but this time work 7 trebles instead of 5 to make yet larger petals. If you need to make a smaller flower than the one we have made, you could finish the flower with this round.

9 Work another round of linking chains as before, working the double crochet round the back of the double crochet worked in the 5th round. Complete the flower with a final layer of petals, working 1 double crochet, 1 half treble, 2 treble, 5 double treble, 2 treble, 1 half treble and a double crochet for each petal.

10 The flower is now complete. You can use on its own by sewing it on to any fabric. If you prefer, enlarge the motif, giving it a granny-square type of background, as shown here. Begin by working the chain loops as before at the back. Work 3 treble, 3 chain and 3 treble into first loop for corner. Work 1 chain, 3 treble and 1 chain into next loop. Repeat alternately into each loop to make 4 corners.

11 On subsequent rounds you will work a corner into each 3 chain space, and a 3-treble group into each 1 chain space with 1 chain at either side, so that on each round you will be increasing a block of trebles on each side of the square. You can continue in this way until the square is as big as you require.

Simple primrose

Here is a much simpler flower which can also be worked with the same background. We have worked only two layers of petals, but you could make more for a larger flower.

1 Make 6 chain and join them into a circle with a slip stitch, as you would when working a square or circular motif. Now begin the first petal by working 1 double crochet, 3 treble and 1 double crochet all into the centre of the ring.

2 Make 2 more petals in exactly the same way and finish the round by joining the last double crochet to the first with a slip stitch. If you are using more than 1 colour, fasten off the yarn at this point by drawing it through the working loop. Make sure that this yarn is kept at the back of the work on following rounds.

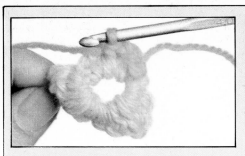

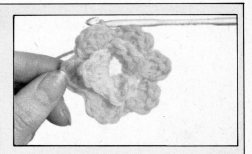

3 Turn the flower over so that the WS is facing you and rejoin the yarn to the back of the first double crochet. Make 3 chain and then work a double crochet into the back of the 2nd (middle) treble of the first petal, passing the hook behind the 2 back loops.

4 Make 3 more chain and work a double crochet round the stem of the 1st double crochet in the 2nd petal. Continue to work 3 chain and a double crochet in this way all the way round the flower so that you finish with six 3-chain loops in all. Join the last chain to the first with a slip stitch to complete the round.

5 Now turn the flower back so that the right side is facing you. (Cut off the yarn here if you wish to change colour and rejoin it to the first loop) Now work a petal into each of the 6 loops in exactly the same way as before. If you wish to make more layers, make another round of chain loops and work into these loops. You may have to increase the size of the petals by working 5 trebles instead of 3.

6 To begin the background turn the flower to the WS again and work a 3 chain loop between each petal, linking the chains by working a double crochet round the stem of the double crochet worked in the previous loop round. You should have 6 loops in all.

7 Now turn the flower to the RS again and make 3 chain for the first treble. Now work 2 treble, 2 chain and 3 treble all into the first loop. Make 1 chain and work 3 treble, 2 chain and 3 treble into each loop all the way round, with 1 chain between each loop, joining the round with a slip stitch.

8 To make the square, either slip stitch across to the first 2-chain space, if you are using the same colour, or join in a new colour to this space. Make 3 chain to count as first treble, then work 2 treble, 3 chain and 3 treble into first space. Work blocks of 3 treble into the two spaces, linked by 1 chain. Work another corner of 3 treble, 3 chain and 3 treble. This sets the pattern.

Fred Mancini

Stitch Wise

Pineapple square.

The flower motif in the centre of this chunky pineapple stitch square is worked into the middle of the square after the square has been completed. By alternating a square with a flower and one without, you could make a very pretty bedcover or rug.

Make 8 chain and join into a circle with a slip stitch.
1st round *(Yrh and insert hook into circle, yrh and draw up a loop) 4 times, yrh and draw it through all 9 loops on hook, called pineapple 4, 2ch; rep from * 7 times more. Join last chain to first pineapple with a ss. 8 pineapples in all.
2nd round Pineapple 4 into 2ch sp before ss, *2ch, pineapple 4 into next sp, 2ch, (1tr, 3ch, 1tr) into top of next pineapple

st, 2ch, pineapple 4 into next sp; rep from *, ending last rep with (1tr, 3ch, 1tr) into next sp, 2ch. Join last ch to first pineapple with a ss.
3rd round Pineapple 4 into sp before ss, *(2ch, pineapple 4) into each sp to corner, 2ch, (1tr, 3ch, 1tr) into corner; rep from * to end, 2ch. Join last ch to first pineapple with a ss.
Rep 3rd round for the size of square required.

To make the flower
Rejoin yarn to any 2ch sp on 1st round. Make 2ch to count as first dc, (yrh and insert hook into same sp, draw up loop) 3 times, yrh and draw through loops on hook, (pineapple 3), 1ch, pineapple 3 in same sp, 1ch, 1dc in same sp, *(1dc, pineapple 3, 1ch, pineapple 3, 1ch, 1dc) all into next 2ch sp in 1st round; rep

from * all round motif. Join last dc to first with a ss. Fasten off.
There should be 8 petals in all.

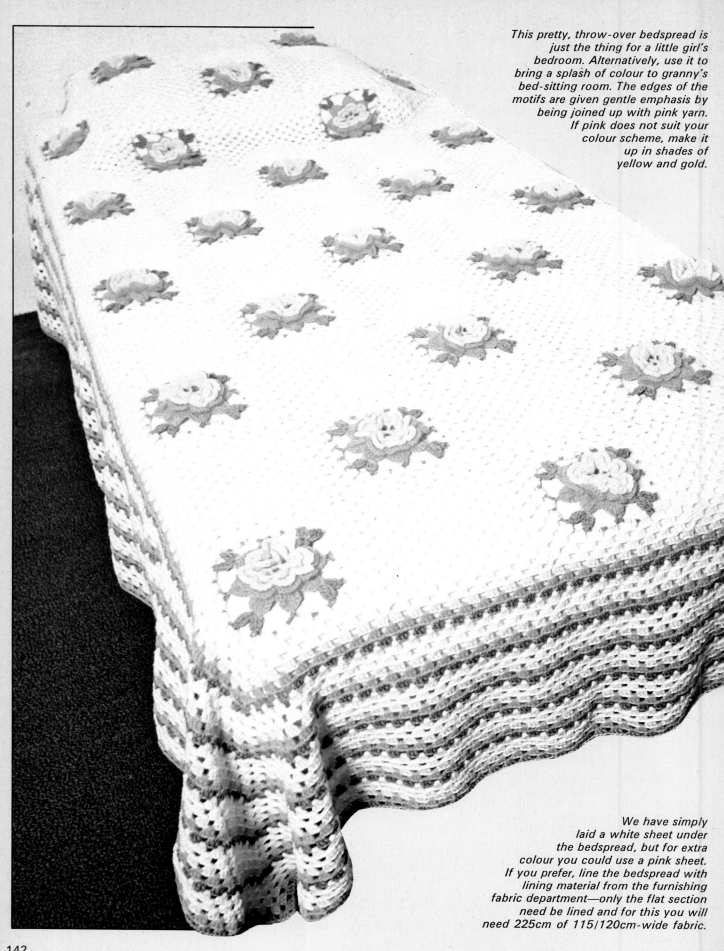

This pretty, throw-over bedspread is just the thing for a little girl's bedroom. Alternatively, use it to bring a splash of colour to granny's bed-sitting room. The edges of the motifs are given gentle emphasis by being joined up with pink yarn. If pink does not suit your colour scheme, make it up in shades of yellow and gold.

We have simply laid a white sheet under the bedspread, but for extra colour you could use a pink sheet. If you prefer, line the bedspread with lining material from the furnishing fabric department—only the flat section need be lined and for this you will need 225cm of 115/120cm-wide fabric.

Everything's coming up roses

This splendid bedspread with its three-dimensional rose motifs will appeal to anyone's romantic nature. The rose motifs are alternated with plain motifs and the border is worked in rounds using each of the colours.

Size
To fit a single bed – 163cm by 230cm approx.

Materials
Wendy Courtellon Double Knit
43 x 20g balls in main colour (A)
17 x 20g balls in 1st contrasting colour (B)
17 x 20g balls in 2nd contrasting colour (C)
10 x 20g balls in 3rd contrasting colour (D)

4.00mm crochet hook

Tension
One motif measures 19cm square.

Rose motif
Using 4.00mm hook and B, make 6ch, join with a ss to first ch to form a ring.
1st round 3ch to count as first tr, *2ch, 1tr into ring, rep from * 6 times more, 2ch, join with a ss to 3rd of first 3ch.
2nd round Work 1dc, 1htr, 3tr, 1htr and 1dc all into each 2ch sp, join with a ss to

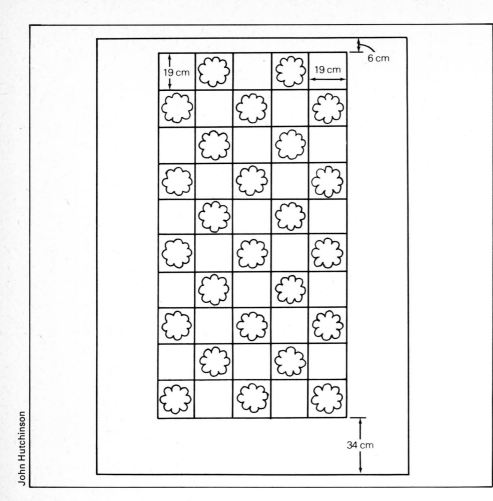

Along the left side: John Hutchinson

Diagram labels: 19 cm, 19 cm, 6 cm, 34 cm

Work 6 more rounds, working 1 more tr group in each round between corner groups, so having six 3tr groups between each corner on last round. Fasten off. Make 24 more squares in the same way.

To make up
Placing motifs as shown in diagram, alternating one rose motif with one plain motif, join the motifs thus : with right sides together, using 4.00mm hook and B and working through the double thickness work 2dc into corner space, *working into the back loops only work 1dc into each of next 3tr, 1dc into next ch sp, rep from * 6 times more, 2dc into corner space. Do not fasten off but continue to join motifs until a row of 10 motifs have been joined. Being very careful not to let the motifs twist, join 4 more rows of motifs. Join the rows of motifs together in the same way.

The border
Working along two long sides and one short end work as folls.
1st row Join B to corner space and using 4.00mm hook work 3ch to count as first tr, 2tr into same space * ch, 3tr into next space, rep from * all round the three edges working 3tr, 3ch and 3tr all into the corner ch spaces.
Fasten off.
2nd row Join on C and working into 3rd ch of first 3ch of previous row work 4ch, *3tr into next 1ch space, 1ch, rep from * all round the 3 edges working 3tr, 3ch and 3tr into the corner ch spaces.
Fasten off.
3rd row Join on D and work as 1st row.
4th row Join on A and work as 2nd row.
5th row Join on A and work as 1st row.
Cont in stripe sequence as set, patt 23 more rows.

Top border
Work in rows along top edge, working 2 rows in A, 1 row in B, 1 row in C and 1 row in D. Fasten off.

Lining
If you wish to line the bedspread, turn in a 2cm double hem all round fabric and slipstitch in place.

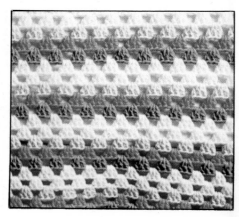

ss at end of first round.
3rd round Keeping each 4ch loop behind the petals of the 2nd round, work *4ch, placing hook from back to front work 1dc round next tr on 1st round, rep from * 6 times more, 4ch, join with a ss to ss at end of previous round.
4th round Work 1dc, 1htr, 5tr, 1htr and 1dc all into each 4ch loop, join with a ss to ss at end of 3rd round.
5th round As 3rd round working into the back of the dc of 3rd round. Cut off B.
6th round Join C to ss at end of last round, work 1dc, 1htr, 7tr, 1htr and 1dc all into each 4ch loop, join with a ss to ss at end of 5th round.
7th round As 3rd round working into the back of the dc of 5th round.
8th round Work 1dc, 1htr, 2tr, 5dtr, 2tr, 1htr and 1dc all into each 4ch loop, join with a ss to ss at end of 7th round. Cut off C.
9th round Join D to centre dtr of one petal, 1ch to count as first dc, then work 7ch, *keeping last loop of each on hook work 3dtr into the centre dtr of next petal, yrh and draw through all 4 loops on hook – called cluster 1 or Cl 1, 4ch, Cl 1 into same st as last Cl 1, 7ch, 1dc into centre dtr of next petal, 7ch, rep from * twice more, work Cl 1, 4ch and Cl 1 all into centre dtr of next petal, 7ch, join with a ss to first ch. Cut off D.

10th round Join A to one corner 4ch space, 3ch to count as first tr, 2tr into corner space, 3ch, 3tr into same space, 1ch, *(3tr, 1ch, 3tr and 1ch all into next 7ch space) twice, 3tr, 3ch, 3tr and 1ch all into corner 4ch space, rep from * twice more, (3tr, 1ch and 3tr all into next 7ch space) twice, join with a ss to 3rd of first 3ch.
11th round Ss over 2tr and into 3ch space, 3ch to count as first tr, 2tr into space, 3ch, 3tr into same space, (1ch, 3tr into next 1ch space) 5 times, *1ch, 3tr, 3ch and 3tr all into corner 3ch space, (1ch, 3tr into next 1ch space) 5 times, rep from * 3 times, 1ch, ss into 3rd of first 3ch.
12th round As 11th round but working six 3tr clusters between each corner.
Fasten off.
Make 24 more motifs in the same way.

Plain motif
Using 4.00mm hook and A, make 6ch, join with a ss to first ch to form a ring.
1st round 3ch to count as first tr, work 2 tr into ring, (3ch, 3tr into ring) 3 times, 3ch, join with a ss to 3rd of first 3ch.
2nd round Ss over next 2tr and into 3ch space, 3ch to count as first tr, work 2tr into same space, 3ch, (1ch, 3tr, 3ch and 3tr all into corner 3ch space) 3 times, 1ch, ss into 3rd of first 3ch.

Index